Briggs, Diane.
101 fingerplays, stories,
and songs to use with
1999.
33305011943911
CA   04/26/99

101

FINGERPLAYS, STORIES, AND SONGS TO USE WITH FINGER PUPPETS

Diane Briggs

American Library Association
Chicago and London

While extensive effort has gone into ensuring the reliability of information appearing in this book, the publisher makes no warranty, express or implied, on the accuracy or reliability of the information, and does not assume and hereby disclaims any liability to any person for any loss or damage caused by errors or omissions in this publication.

Project editor: Joan A. Grygel

Cover: Baugher Design

Text design: Dianne M. Rooney

Composition by the dotted i in Garamond using QuarkXPress 3.32

Printed on 60-pound Finch Opaque, a pH-neutral stock, and bound in 10-point coated cover stock by Edwards Brothers

The paper used in this publication meets the minimum requirements of American National Standard for Information Sciences—Permanence of Paper for Printed Library Materials, ANSI Z39.48–1992. ∞

Library of Congress Cataloging-in-Publication Data

Briggs, Diane.
    101 fingerplays, stories, and songs to use with finger puppets / by Diane Briggs.
        p.   cm.
    ISBN 0-8389-0749-0
    1. Finger play.   2. Finger puppets.   I. Title.
    GV1218.F5B74   1999
    791.5′3—dc21   98-42136

Copyright © 1999 by the American Library Association. All rights reserved except those which may be granted by Sections 107 and 108 of the Copyright Revision Act of 1976.

Printed in the United States of America.

03 02 01 00 99   5 4 3 2 1

To Mom, Dad,
and my wonderful sisters,
Brenda and Ellen

CONTENTS

PREFACE

During more than twelve years as a children's and school librarian, I've witnessed how children of all ages react to puppets—they simply adore them. I used to keep finger puppet gloves on my desk at school, but I eventually found that I had to put them in a drawer because the children would invariably start a puppet show when I wasn't looking. Many times when I present a finger puppet story, a chorus requests me to "tell it again," and many children beg for a chance to tell the story themselves. Finger puppets appeal to children of all ages. They can be used with babies, toddlers, preschoolers, and children in the early elementary grades. In fact, older children love to do finger puppet stories for the younger children during special finger puppet programs. For example, a unit that combines art and language could teach older children how to make attractive finger puppets and give them the opportunity to perform stories for younger children in the school. Such activities could also be offered in after-school programs, day care centers, preschools, and hospitals.

I came to the idea for *101 Fingerplays, Stories, and Songs to Use with Finger Puppets* when searching for resource materials on finger puppets to use in my storytimes. I found a number of good books on puppetry in general but virtually nothing on finger puppets. Using finger puppets is an easy and practical way to enliven your storytime programs with puppetry. Presented here are many rhymes, stories, and songs from traditional folklore and a few selections that I have written or adapted. I have intentionally drawn the patterns in a basic style so it will be easier for you to make the felt puppets.

Librarians have a constant need for new program materials, and this book provides an abundance of ideas that can be used in many ways. The selections in this book may be used not only for finger puppets but can just as easily be used to create flannel board presentations, stick puppets, or ideas for theme programs.

ACKNOWLEDGMENTS

I'd like to thank all the librarians and storytellers in my life from whom I've learned so much. I'm especially grateful to my friends Lisa Bouchard of the Bethlehem Public Library and Lisa Renz of the Utica Public Library who have always given me encouragement and help whenever I've needed it. I'd also like to thank my husband, Scott, who is also a librarian and is always there with intelligent input. Finally, many thanks go to ALA Editions and my editor Patrick Hogan.

INTRODUCTION

*E*ach of the 101 fingerplays, stories, and songs in this book includes patterns for making the individual puppets and props. In addition, specific directions for the puppet actions are given. Book lists are included that relate to the themes of the finger puppet rhymes, stories, or songs. The carefully selected titles are a combination of classics and books of recent copyright. A full bibliography is provided at the end of the book. In addition, a discography of songs will help you locate a recording of a tune if you are unfamiliar with it. The rhymes, stories, and songs in this book have been collected from folklore or written by myself unless otherwise indicated.

FINGER PUPPET GLOVES

The finger puppet activities in this book are designed to be used with felt puppets attached to the fingertips of a glove. Use your imagination when you choose a glove to use with your puppets. You can use inexpensive garden gloves, rubber household gloves, different colored gloves, glittery gloves, or red and green gloves for a Christmas theme. You could also paint a special story scene on a white cotton glove. Above all make sure the glove fits fairly snugly. Glove fingers that are too big or long may cause the puppets to flop over. Decide which hand you want to use for storytelling, and sew Velcro to the fingertips on both sides of the glove so you may use either side of the glove depending on the rhyme or story. For example, when a story calls for the fingers to be folded down one by one, the back of your hand should be facing the audience. Therefore, you will need to place the puppets over your fingernails. Take special care when you sew the Velcro on the thumb. The side of the thumb usually faces front when you hold your hand up. Double-stick tape may be used successfully instead of Velcro, but tape has the disadvantage of not being permanent.

USING THE PATTERNS

Patterns are provided to use with each of the fingerplays, stories, and songs. The simple lines make it easier for you to trace the patterns. In addition to their use for making finger puppets, the patterns can be used to make flannel board figures, stick puppets, or bulletin boards. The following sections provide detailed directions for using the patterns in each of these ways.

Finger Puppets

You may use the patterns to make puppets out of felt. The vibrant colors of felt that are available in craft stores will make the most-attractive puppets. To make felt puppets, photocopy the pattern. Then pin or tape it to felt, and cut around the edges. Make as many of the puppets as needed for the activities. (For example, make five bears for "Five Brown Teddies.") Remove the paper and add wiggle eyes and felt details to the felt cutout. A fine-point permanent marker may be used to indicate lines. Be creative in decorating the puppets. Use fake fur, craft hair, sequins, beads, craft feathers, or anything else that catches your fancy.

Simple, flat felt puppets work fine. However, if you prefer a more three-dimensional finger puppet, cut out two layers of felt for each pattern, join the edges with hot glue, or sew them, and put in a little stuffing. Glue Velcro (fuzzy, loop side) to the puppets, and attach them to Velcro tabs (rough, hook side) on the glove. Double-stick tape may be used instead of Velcro. In fact, double-stick tape is preferred for rhymes in which the puppets are removed from the glove. In this way, you avoid the distracting "ripping" sound of Velcro. Double-stick tape can be used right over Velcro if you've already sewn or glued Velcro to the glove or puppets.

If you choose to make the puppets out of paper, simply photocopy the patterns, color them, cut them out, and cover them with a clear adhesive. Add wiggle eyes and glue the Velcro or use double-stick tape as directed for felt puppets.

Flannel Board Figures

The puppets for the stories, rhymes, and songs in this book are directly transferable to use with a flannel board. Enlarge the patterns on a photocopier, pin them to felt, and cut them out. Remove the paper and add details to the felt figures as described for the puppets, except do not use stuffing. You may want to make some additional props for individual rhymes. For example, make a beehive for "Here Is the Beehive."

Stick Puppets

If you wish to make stick puppets, enlarge the patterns on a photocopier to an appropriate size. Trace the patterns onto poster board or heavy paper. Color the puppets and decorate them, then cover them with clear adhesive. Attach a stick to the back of the puppet. Use the puppets behind a theater or let children hold them and perform the actions as you tell the story or rhyme.

Bulletin Board Figures

To use the patterns for a bulletin board, enlarge them on a photocopier, then trace them onto fabric or paper. Color the traced patterns, cut them out, and decorate them.

STORYTELLING TIPS

Be sure the puppets and props are ready and organized before you begin your storytime. If you will be placing the puppets on your fingers in a particular order during storytelling, as for "The Little Red Hen" or "The Gingerbread Boy," arrange them sequentially in advance and place them in a small box that you can keep on your lap or nearby. This box may also be used to put puppets in if you are removing them from the glove during a rhyme or story.

To ease the pressure of memorizing, photocopy the rhymes in reduced sized print. Attach the rhymes to the back of your glove with double-stick tape for ready reference.

It may be wise to put the puppet glove out of sight when you've finished a story so the children aren't distracted by it when you begin the next activity or story.

Bears

Five Brown Teddies
—Traditional nursery song

(See discography for tune)

Five brown teddies sitting on a wall,
Five brown teddies sitting on a wall,
If one brown teddy should accidentally fall,
There'd be four brown teddies sitting on a wall.

Four brown teddies . . .

Three brown teddies . . .

Two brown teddies . . .

One brown teddy . . . There'd be no brown teddies. . . .

Bears in a Cave
—Folk rhyme

Here is a cave.
Inside there are bears.
Now they come out
To get some fresh air.

They stay out all summer
In sunshine and heat.
And hunt in the forest
For berries to eat.

When the snow starts to fall,
They hurry inside
Their warm little cave,
And there they will hide.

Snow covers the cave
Like a fluffy white rug.
Inside the bears sleep,
All cozy and snug.

This Little Teddy
—Adapted folk rhyme

This little teddy has a soft furry suit.
This little teddy is sweet and cute.
This little teddy is sassy and cross.
This little teddy thinks she's the boss.
This little teddy likes berries and honey,
But when he gets them on his face,
He looks very, very funny.

PREPARATION

Make five bears.

PUPPETRY DIRECTIONS

Five Brown Teddies

Make a small wall out of poster board to hold underneath the teddies and in front of your gloved hand. The teddies should be placed on the Velcro tabs over your fingernails. The back of your hand should face listeners. Fold each finger down on cue starting with your thumb, then your little finger (hold it down with your thumb), ring finger, and so on.

Bears in a Cave

Close your gloved hand and hide the puppets in your fist as if they are in a cave. Pop them up when they come out. Close your hand again and cover it with your other hand to indicate snow on the cave.

This Little Teddy

Perform this rhyme with your fingers in an upright position and put each bear on the glove one at a time as you say the rhyme.

RELATED BOOKS

Alborough, Jez. *Where's My Teddy.*
Cartwright, Stephen. *Find the Teddy.*
Galdone, Paul. *The Three Bears.*
Kasza, Keiko. *A Mother for Choco.*
Kozikowski, Renate. *The Teddy Bear's Picnic.*
Manzsell, Dom. *My Old Teddy.*
Rosen, Michael. *We're Going on a Bear Hunt.*
Stevens, Janet. *Tops and Bottoms.*
Waddell, Martin. *Can't You Sleep, Little Bear?*
Young, Ruth. *Golden Bear.*

Birds

Five Pretty Blue Birds
—Adapted folk rhyme

Five pretty blue birds singing so sweet,
The first pretty blue bird said, "Tweet, tweet, tweet."
The second pretty blue bird started to sing,
The third pretty blue bird flapped its wings.
The fourth pretty blue bird sat in its nest,
The fifth pretty blue bird said, "Springtime is best!"
Then all the little blue birds on that glorious day,
Spread out their wings and flew away!

Two Little Red Birds
—Mother Goose

Two little red birds
Sitting on a hill.
One named Jack,
One named Jill.
Fly away, Jack,
Fly away, Jill,
Come back, Jack,
Come back, Jill.
Two little red birds
Sitting on a hill.

Five Little Birds

—Adapted folk rhyme

Five little birds peeping at the door,
The yellow one flew away, and that
    left four.
Four little birds sitting in a tree,
The blue one flew away, and
    that left three.
Three little birds looking
    at you,
The black one flew away, and
    that left two.
Two little birds sitting in the sun,
The brown one flew away, and that
    left one.
One little red bird left all alone,
It flew away, and that left none.

PREPARATION

Make ten birds: five blue, two red, and one each yellow, black, and brown.

PUPPETRY DIRECTIONS

Five Pretty Bluebirds

Begin this rhyme with the fingers upright. Put each bird on a finger as it appears in the rhyme (the "first," the "second," and so on). Hide the birds behind your back at the end of the rhyme.

Two Little Red Birds

Place a bird on each index finger. Use double-stick tape on your bare fingers if desired. When each bird flies away, hide it behind your back. Bring each out again on cue.

Five Little Birds

Start this rhyme with all the birds on the glove. Remove each bird from your glove when it flies away.

RELATED BOOKS

Asch, Frank. *Bear's Bargain.*

Ehlert, Lois. *Feathers for Lunch.*

Graham, Margaret Bloy. *Benjy and the Barking Bird.*

Hutchins, Pat. *Good-Night Owl.*

Meddaugh, Susan. *Tree of Birds.*

Pilkey, Dav. *The Silly Gooses.*

Troughton, Joanna. *How the Birds Changed Their Feathers.*

Van Laan, Nancy. *The Big Fat Worm.*

Waddell, Martin. *Owl Babies.*

Wood, Audrey. *Birdsong.*

Bugs

Five Little Ladybugs

Five little ladybugs sitting on a
    flower.
One flew away when it began
    to shower.
Four little ladybugs crawling on a
    tree.
One flew away, and that left
    three.
Three little ladybugs walking
    on you.
One flew away, and then there were
    two.
Two little ladybugs resting in the sun.
One flew away, and that left one.
One little ladybug flew away home.
She didn't want her children to be all alone.

Busy Bugs

Five little busy bugs playing on the floor,
Pussy cat grabbed one, then there were four.
Four little busy bugs playing on a tree,
One chased a buzzy fly, then there were three.
Three little busy bugs looked for flowers new,
A turkey gobbler saw them, then there were two.
Two little busy bugs sitting in the sun,
A hoppy toad spied them, then there was one.
One little busy bug left all alone,
He flapped his tiny wings and flew on home.

Here Is the Beehive

—Folk rhyme

Here is the beehive.
Where are the bees?
Hidden inside where nobody sees.
Here they all come buzzing from the hive,
One, two, three,
Four, and five!

Baby Bumble Bee

—Traditional nursery rhyme

(See discography for tune)

Oh, I'm bringing home a baby bumble bee.
Won't my mommy be so proud of me
'Cause I'm bringing home a baby bumble bee?
Buzzy, buzzy, buzzy.
Oh, it stung me!

PREPARATION

Make five ladybugs and five bees. Make the antennae and legs out of paper or dip small pieces of string in glue to make them stiff. Glue tiny beads to the ends of the antennae. A fine-point permanent marker may be used to indicate lines or dots.

PUPPETRY DIRECTIONS

Five Little Ladybugs and Busy Bugs

Start the rhymes with the bugs on the glove. Remove them from the glove one by one as they fly away.

Here Is the Beehive

Start the rhyme with all the bees hidden in your gloved hand. Your hand should be in a fist. Then pop the bees up one at a time as you count.

Baby Bumble Bee

> Place one bee on your index finger. Dance it around a little as you sing. At the end of the song pretend that it stings you on the arm, cheek, or elsewhere.

FLANNEL BOARD ADAPTATION

> For "Here is the Beehive," cut a beehive shape out of brown or gray felt.

RELATED BOOKS

Aylesworth, Jim. *Old Black Fly.*

Carle, Eric. *The Grouchy Ladybug.*

Fleming, Denise. *In the Tall, Tall Grass.*

Hall, Katy. *Buggy Riddles.*

Kennedy, Kim. *Mr. Bumble.*

Kent, Jack. *The Caterpillar and the Polliwog.*

McDonald, Megan. *Insects Are My Life.*

Van Allsburg, Chris. *Two Bad Ants.*

West, Colin. *"Buzz, Buzz, Buzz," Went Bumblebee.*

Yoshi. *Butterfly Hunt.*

Bunnies

Bunny in a Hat

A little soft bunny,
With fur as white as snow,
Will magically appear,
When I wave my wand like so.
Abracadabra! Alacazam!
Come out of the hat little bunny,
Show us you can!

My Bunnies

—Adapted folk rhyme

"The bunnies now must go to bed,"
The furry mother bunny said.
"But I must count them first to see
If they have all come back to me.
One bunny, two bunnies, three
    bunnies dear,
Four bunnies, five bunnies—
    yes, they're all here.
They are the prettiest things
    alive,
My bunnies, one, two, three, four,
    five."

Bunny in a Hole
—Folk rhyme

A bunny lived in a little hole,
Lived softly in a little hole,
When all was quiet as quiet can be . . .
Out popped he!

Here Is a Bunny
—Folk rhyme

Here is a bunny with ears so funny,
And here is her hole in the ground.
When a noise she hears, she pricks up her ears,
And hops in her hole in the ground.

PREPARATION

For "Bunny in a Hat," use the pattern to make a small black hat out of felt. Back it with poster board to make it stiff. Make five bunnies.

PUPPETRY DIRECTIONS

Bunny in a Hat

Put a bunny puppet on your index finger and hold the hat in front of it. Make the bunny pop up on cue.

My Bunnies

Start this rhyme with the fingers in an upright position. Put the bunnies on your fingers one by one as they are counted by the mother bunny in the rhyme.

Bunny in a Hole

Put a bunny on your index finger and hide it in your fist. Let it pop up at the end of the rhyme.

Here Is a Bunny

Put a bunny on your index finger and hold it upright. With your other hand form a circle (the bunny's hole) by touching your index finger to your thumb. Hop the bunny into the hole at the end of the rhyme.

RELATED BOOKS

Aardema, Verna. *Rabbit Makes a Monkey Out of Lion*.

Brown, Margaret Wise. *Goodnight Moon*.

———. *The Runaway Bunny*.

Denim, Sue. *The Dumb Bunnies*.

Jewell, Nancy. *Snuggle Bunny*.

McBratney, Sam. *Guess How Much I Love You*.

Potter, Beatrix. *Tale of Peter Rabbit*.

Van Leeuwen, Jean. *Emma Bean*.

Wells, Rosemary. *Bunny Cakes*.

Zolotow, Charlotte. *Mr. Rabbit and the Lovely Present*.

Chicken Little

—Traditional nursery tale

PREPARATION

Make one puppet from each pattern.

PUPPETRY DIRECTIONS

Memorize a version of "Chicken Little," such as *Chicken Little* by Sally Hobson. Start the story with the fingers in an upright position. Place each puppet on a finger when characters make their entrances in the story. Since there are seven characters in the story you will need two gloves. The last two characters to appear (Turkey Lurkey and Foxy Loxy) should be already in place on the second glove. Slip the glove on quickly when you've finished putting the other characters on the first glove. Pop the last two characters up on cue. To show that the fox had them all for dinner, hide the puppets behind your back when the story ends.

RELATED BOOKS

Conrad, Pam. *The Rooster's Gift.*

Ernst, Lisa Campbell. *Zinnia and Dot.*

French, Vivian. *Red Hen and Sly Fox.*

Galdone, Paul. *Henny Penny.*

————. *Little Tuppen.*

Ginsburg, Mirra. *Good Morning, Chick.*

Hobson, Sally. *Chicken Little.*

Hutchins, Pat. *Rosie's Walk.*

Ormerod, Jan. *The Story of Chicken Licken.*

Rader, Laura. *Chicken Little.*

Chicks

The Little Chick
—Folk rhyme

A perfect white egg sat on by Mother Hen
To keep it warm and then,
Crack, crack, crack,
Peep, peep, peep,
A baby chick softly cheeps.

Little Chicks' Bedtime
—Folk rhyme

"My little chicks now must go to bed,"
The big mother hen said.
"But I will count them first to see,
If they have all come back to me.
Here a chick, there a chick, three chicks dear,
Four chicks, five chicks—yes, all are here.
They are the sweetest things alive,
My little chicks one, two, three, four,
    five."

Five Little Chickens
—Traditional English rhyme

Said the first little chicken
With a queer little squirm,
"Oh, I wish I could find
A fat little worm!"

Said the second little chicken
With an odd little shrug,
"Oh, I wish I could find
A fat little bug!"

Said the third little chicken
With a little sigh of grief,
"Oh, I wish I could find
A green little leaf!"

Said the fourth little chicken
With a sharp little squeal.
"Oh, I wish I could find
Some nice yellow meal!"

Said the fifth little chicken
With a faint little moan
"Oh, I wish I could find
A wee gravel stone!"

"Now see here," said their mother,
From the green garden patch,
"If you want any breakfast,
You must come here and scratch!"

PREPARATION

Make five chicks. For "The Little Chick" enlarge the egg pattern and make an egg out of poster board. Connect the pieces with a brad.

PUPPETRY DIRECTIONS

The Little Chick

Hold the poster board egg (closed) in front of a finger puppet chick. "Crack" open the egg and pop the chick up at the end of the rhyme.

Little Chicks' Bedtime and Five Little Chickens

> Start these rhymes with the fingers in an upright position. Put the chicks on the fingers one by one. For "Little Chicks' Bedtime" place chicks on the fingers as the chicks are counted by the mother hen. For "Five Little Chickens" put each chick on a finger as it says its line. You can play the part of the mother hen by wagging your finger at the chicks during the last verse.

FLANNEL BOARD ADAPTATION

> If desired, enlarge the hen pattern from "Farm Animals" to play the part of Mother Hen. For "Five Little Chickens" make the little items the chicks want to eat out of felt and place them on their beaks at the end of the rhyme.

RELATED BOOKS

Auch, Mary Jane. *Easter Egg Farm.*
———. *Peeping Beauty.*
Ginsburg, Mirra. *Across the Stream.*
———. *The Chick and the Duckling.*
Heine, Helme. *The Most Wonderful Egg in the World.*
Kasza, Keiko. *The Wolf's Chicken Stew.*
Kent, Jack. *Little Peep.*
Pomerantz, Charlotte. *Here Comes Henny.*
Williams, Garth. *The Chicken Book.*

Clowns

This Little Clown

This little clown has a round red nose.
This little clown can dance on her toes.
This little clown is a jolly good
    fellow.
This little clown wears a hat that's
    yellow.
And this little clown is wee and
    small.
But he can walk the tightrope and
    never fall.

Five Little Funny Clowns

Five little funny clowns with magic
    tricks galore,
One disappeared, and then there
    were four.
Four little funny clowns doing flips
    for me,
One fell down, and then there
    were three.
Three little funny clowns with big
    enormous shoes,
One ran away, and then there were
    two.
Two little funny clowns were having such fun,
One fell off the tightrope, and then there was one.
One little funny clown performing like a hero,
She left the circus, and then there were zero.

PREPARATION

Make one of each clown. One clown should have a yellow hat.

PUPPETRY DIRECTIONS

This Little Clown

Start this rhyme with the fingers in an upright position. Place the clowns on the fingers one by one on cue.

Five Funny Little Clowns

Start this rhyme with the clowns on the fingers. Remove each clown at the appropriate time.

RELATED BOOKS

Blume, Karin. *Circus: Funny Fingers.*

Burningham, John. *Cannonball Simp.*

Drescher, Henrik. *Klutz.*

Ehlert, Lois. *Circus.*

Ernst, Lisa Campbell. *Ginger Jumps.*

Freeman, Don. *Bearymore.*

London, Jonathan. *Little Red Monkey.*

Paxton, Tom. *Engelbert Joins the Circus.*

Peet, Bill. *Chester the Worldly Pig.*

Wildsmith, Brian. *The Circus.*

Cookies

Five Little Cookies
—Adapted folk rhyme

Five little cookies with frosting galore,
Mommy ate the white one, then there were four.
Four little cookies, two and two you see,
Daddy ate the pink one, then there were three.
Three little cookies, but before I knew,
My sister ate the blue one, then there were two.
Two little cookies, oh, what fun!
My brother ate the green one, then there was one.
One little cookie, watch me run!
I ate the red one, then there were none.

Five Little Cookies in a Bakery
—Adapted folk rhyme

Five little cookies in a bakery shop,
Shining bright with sugar on top.
Along came *(insert child's name)* with
    a penny one day,
And bought a cookie and ran
    away.

Four little cookies . . .

Three little cookies . . .

Two little cookies . . .

One little cookie . . .

PREPARATION

Make one cookie in each of the following colors: white, pink, blue, green, and red.

PUPPETRY DIRECTIONS

Start each rhyme with the cookies on the fingers. Remove the cookies one by one according to the rhyme.

RELATED BOOKS

Hoban, Lillian. *Arthur's Christmas Cookies.*

Hooper, Meredith. *A Cow, a Bee, a Cookie and Me.*

Hutchins, Pat. *The Doorbell Rang.*

Lindgren, Barbro. *Sam's Cookie.*

Marx, Patricia. *Joey T. and the Missing Cookie: A Lift-the-Flap Adventure.*

Rix, Jamie. *The Last Chocolate Cookie.*

Robart, Rose. *The Cake That Mack Ate.*

Sabuda, Robert. *Cookie Count: A Tasty Pop-Up Book.*

Wellington, Monica. *Mr. Cookie Baker.*

Dinosaurs

The Teeny Tiny Dinosaurs

Five teeny tiny dinosaurs lived in a time long ago,
First one said, "I'm the biggest, you know."
Second one said, "I can roar louder than you."
Third one said, "I can eat a ton of leaves too."
Fourth one said, "I have spikes on my head."
Fifth one said, "Mommy's calling. It's time for bed."

Five Little Dinosaurs
—Adapted nursery rhyme

(Tune: "Five Little Frogs," see discography)

Five little dinosaurs,
Let out a great big roar,
And ate up some most delicious bugs.
Yum! Yum!
One jumped into a pool,
Where it was nice and cool,
Then there were four little dinosaurs.
Roar, roar.

(repeat with 4, 3, 2, and 1)

No little dinosaurs.

PREPARATION

Make five dinosaurs.

PUPPETRY DIRECTIONS

The Teeny Tiny Dinosaurs

Start this rhyme with the fingers in an upright position. Place the dinosaurs on the fingers one by one on cue.

Five Little Dinosaurs

Before beginning this song, place the dinosaurs on the fingers. As you sing the song, remove one dinosaur each verse.

RELATED BOOKS

Cauley, Lorinda Bryan. *The Trouble with Tyrannosaurus Rex.*

Grambling, Lois G. *Can I Have a Stegosaurus, Mom? Can I? Please!?*

Hartman, Wendy. *The Dinosaurs Are Back and It's Your Fault, Edward!*

Most, Bernard. *How Big Were the Dinosaurs?*

Murphy, Jim. *Dinosaur for a Day.*

Schwartz, Henry. *How I Captured a Dinosaur.*

Sierra, Judy. *Good Night, Dinosaurs.*

Torres, Daniel. *Tom.*

Weatherby, Mark Allan. *My Dinosaur.*

Dogs

This Little Puppy
—Folk rhyme

This little puppy said, "Let's go out to play,"
This little puppy said, "Let's run away,"
This little puppy said, "Let's stay out till dark,"
This little puppy said, "Let's bark, bark, bark,"
This little puppy said, "I think it would be fun
To go straight home, so let's run, run, run."

Five Little Puppy Dogs
—Adapted folk rhyme

Five little puppy dogs by the kitchen door,
One left the crowd, then there were
    four.
Four little puppy dogs running
    round a tree,
Mommy called one home, then there
    were three.
Three little puppy dogs
    playing with a shoe,
One ran after a cat, then
    there were two.
Two little puppy dogs having
    so much fun,
One went to find a bone, then there
    was one.
One little puppy dog sitting in the sun,
She went in the kitchen, then there were none.

Where Has My Little Dog Gone?

—Traditional nursery song

(See discograpy for tune)

Oh where, oh where has my little dog gone?
Oh where, oh where can he be?
With his ears cut short,
And his tail cut long,
Oh where, oh where can he be?
Oh! Here he is!

PREPARATION

Make five dogs.

PUPPETRY DIRECTIONS

This Little Puppy

Begin this rhyme with the fingers in an upright position. Put on each dog one by one as you say the rhyme.

Five Little Puppy Dogs

Start this rhyme with the puppets on the fingers. Remove them one by one on cue.

Where Has My Little Dog Gone?

Put a dog on your index finger and fold it into your fist. At the end of the song pop it up.

RELATED BOOKS

Brown, Ken. *Mucky Pup.*

Flack, Marjorie. *Angus and the Cat.*

Golembe, Carla. *Dog Magic.*

Gregory, Nan. *How Smudge Came.*

Hall, Martin. *Charlie and Tess.*

Hazen, Barbara. *The New Dog.*

Hurd, Thacher. *Art Dog.*

Rey, Margaret. *Pretzel.*

Stern, Simon. *The Hobyas: An Old Story.*

Zion, Gene. *Harry the Dirty Dog.*

Ducks

Five Little Ducks Went in for a Swim
—Folk rhyme

Five little ducks went in for a swim;
The first little duck put his head in.
The second little duck put his head back;
The third little duck said, "Quack, quack,
    quack."
The fourth little duck with his tiny brother,
Went for a walk with his father and mother.

Funny Ducks

This funny duck went waddle, waddle, waddle.
This funny duck went paddle, paddle, paddle.
This funny duck went "Quack, quack, quack."
This funny duck wiggled its tail in the back.
And this funny duck, the very last,
Jumped in the water and went splash, splash, splash!

Five Little Ducks

—Traditional song

(See discography for tune)

Five little ducks went out one day
Over the hills and far away.
Mother duck said, "Quack, quack,
    quack, quack!"
But only four little ducks came
    back.

(repeat with 4, 3, 2, 1)

. . . But no little ducks came back.

Sad mother duck went out one day
Over the hills and far away.
Mother duck said, "Quack, quack, quack,
    quack."
And all of the five little ducks came back!

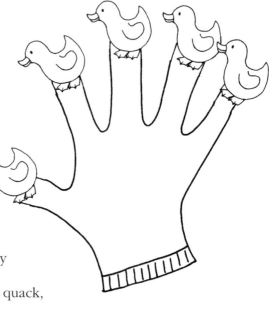

PREPARATION

Make five ducks. Add wiggle eyes, small craft feathers, and felt details
to the felt cutouts.

PUPPETRY DIRECTIONS

Five Little Ducks Went in for a Swim and Funny Ducks

Start these rhymes with the fingers in an upright position. Place the
ducks on the fingers one by one on cue as you recite the rhymes.

Five Little Ducks

Before beginning this song put the ducks on your fingers. At the end of
each verse hide the ducks behind your back and fold one duck down
each time. Bring your hand back out to show that one duck didn't
come back. When down to no little ducks, leave hand behind your
back and shake your head to show that the ducks didn't come back. At
the end of the song, pop up all the ducks.

RELATED BOOKS

Arnosky, Jim. *All Night Near the Water.*

Bunting, Eve. *Ducky.*

Dabcovich, Lydia. *Ducks Fly.*

Delton, Judy. *Two Good Friends.*

Primavera, Elise. *The Three Dots.*

Silverman, Erica. *Don't Fidget a Feather.*

Simmons, Jane. *Come along, Daisy!*

Tafuri, Nancy. *Have You Seen My Duckling.*

Verbven, Agnes. *Ducks Like to Swim.*

Waddell, Martin. *Farmer Duck.*

Elephants

Five Tiny Elephants
—Adapted folk rhyme

Five tiny elephants playing near the shore,
One fell in the water, and that left four.
Four tiny elephants climbing up a tree,
One slid down the trunk, and that left three.
Three tiny elephants living in a zoo,
One walked out the gate, and that left two.
Two tiny elephants having tons of fun,
One went to take a bath, and that left one.
One tiny elephant sitting in the sun,
He chased a butterfly, and that left none.

The Elephant Goes
—Folk rhyme

The elephant goes like this and that.
He's terribly big,
And he's terribly fat,
He has no fingers,
He has no toes,
But goodness, gracious,
What a nose!

The Elephant
—Folk rhyme

The elephant looks like a giant.
He is wrinkled and he is strong.
He has two big floppy ears,
And a nose that's oh so long.
He sways back and forth
Through the jungle he goes
With his big floppy ears
And his hose of a nose.

PREPARATION

Make five elephants from the first pattern (side view) and one from the second pattern. For "The Elephant Goes" and "The Elephant," enlarge the pattern on a photocopier to about five or six inches tall. Cut out the trunk hole. Add wiggle eyes.

PUPPETRY DIRECTIONS

Five Tiny Elephants

Before beginning this rhyme place the elephants on the glove. Remove the elephants one by one according to the rhyme.

The Elephant Goes and The Elephant

While you recite these rhymes put your finger through the trunk hole and move your finger around to simulate the movements of an elephant's trunk. This puppet also makes an ideal craft for the end of a story program.

RELATED BOOKS

Ford, Miela. *Little Elephant.*

McKee, David. *Elmer.*

————. *Elmer Again.*

Murphy, Jill. *A Quiet Night In.*

Riddel, Chris. *The Trouble with Elephants.*

Sierra, Judy. *The Elephant's Wrestling Match.*

Tompert, Ann. *Just a Little Bit.*

Vipont, Elfrida. *The Elephant and the Bad Baby.*

Westcott, Nadine Bernard. *Peanut Butter and Jelly.*

Young, Ed. *Seven Blind Mice.*

Farm Animals

I Had a Little Rooster
—Folk song

(See discography for tune)

I had a little rooster by the barnyard gate,
And that little rooster was my playmate,
And that little rooster sang, "Cock-a-doodle-doo,
A doodley, doodley, doodley-doo."

I had a hen by the barnyard gate,
And that little hen was my playmate,
And that little hen sang, "Cluck, cluck,
    cluck,"
And that little rooster sang, "Cock-a-
    doodle-doo,
A doodley, doodley, doodley-doo."

I had a little cow by the barnyard gate,
And that little cow was my playmate,
And that little cow sang, "Mooo, moo,"
And that little hen sang, "Cluck, cluck, cluck,"
And that little rooster sang, "Cock-a-
    doodle-doo,
A doodley, doodley, doodley-doo."

I had a little dog by the barnyard gate,
And that little dog was my playmate,
And that little dog sang, "Woof, woof,
    woof,"
And that little cow sang, "Mooo, moo,"
And that little hen sang, "Cluck, cluck, cluck,"
And that little rooster sang, "Cock-a-doodle-doo,
A doodley, doodley, doodley-doo."

I had a little cat by the barnyard gate,
And that little cat was my playmate,
And that little cat sang, "Meow, meow, meow,"
And that little dog sang, "Woof, woof, woof,"
And that little cow sang, "Mooo, moo,"
And that little hen sang, "Cluck, cluck, cluck,"
And that little rooster sang, "Cock-a-doodle-doo,
A doodley, doodley, doodley-doo."

Fiddle-I-Fee
—Folk song

(See discography for tune)

I had a cat and the cat pleased me,
I fed my cat under yonder tree.
Cat goes fiddle-i-fee.

I had a hen . . . *(repeat as above)*
Hen goes chimmy chuck, chimmy chuck,
Cat goes fiddle-i-fee.

I had a duck . . . *(repeat as above)*
Duck goes quack, quack,
Hen goes chimmy chuck, chimmy chuck,
Cat goes fiddle-i-fee.

I had a pig . . . *(repeat as above)*
Pig goes oink, oink,
Duck goes quack, quack,
Hen goes chimmy chuck, chimmy chuck,
Cat goes fiddle-i-fee.

I had a cow . . . *(repeat as above)*
Cow goes moo, moo,
Pig goes oink, oink,
Duck goes quack, quack,
Hen goes chimmy chuck, chimmy chuck,
Cat goes fiddle-i-fee.

Farm Animal Friends
—Folk rhyme

This is hungry Piggy Snout,
He'd better stop eating or his tail will pop out.
This is busy Mother Hen,

She likes to scratch for her chickens ten.
This is patient Friendly Cow,
She likes to eat from a big haymow.
This funny duck we call "Quack,"
Likes to ruffle the feathers on his back.
And this is little Fuzzy Cat,
She likes to chase a mouse or rat.

PREPARATION

Make one of each pattern.

PUPPETRY DIRECTIONS

Begin each song or rhyme with the fingers in an upright position. Put each animal on a finger as they make their entrance during the song or rhyme. Point to them or wiggle them when you make each animal sound. Encourage the children to join in on the animal sound effects.

Fiddle-I-Fee

Use the puppet cat with the fiddle.

RELATED BOOKS

Allen, Pamela. *Belinda*.
Berkowitz, Linda. *Alfonse, Where Are You?*
Brown, Margaret Wise. *Big Red Barn*.
Ehlert, Lois. *Color Farm*.
Harrison, David L. *When Cows Come Home*.
Hill, Eric. *Spot Goes to the Farm*.
King, Bob. *Sitting on the Farm*.
McDonnell, Flora. *I Love Animals*.
Most, Bernard. *Cock-a-Doddle-Moo!*
Nodset, Joan L. *Who Took the Farmer's Hat*.
Wood, Jakki. *Moo, Moo, Brown Cow*.

Finger People

Tommy Thumb
—Folk rhyme

This is little Tommy Thumb,
Round and smooth as any plum.
This is busy Peter Pointer,
Surely he's a double-jointer.
This is mighty Toby Tall,
He's the biggest one of all.
This is dainty Rhonda Ring,
She's too fine for anything.
And this little wee one maybe,
Is the pretty Finger Baby!

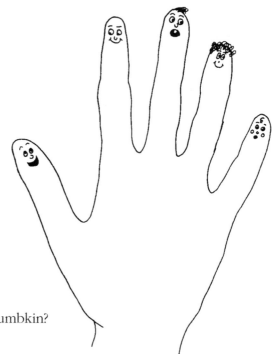

Where Is Thumbkin?
—Traditional song

(See discography for tune)

Where is Thumbkin? Where is Thumbkin?
Here I am. Here I am.
How are you this morning?
Very well, I thank you.
Run and play. Run and play.

Where is Pointer? Where is Pointer?
(repeat as above)

Where is Tall Man? Where is Tall Man?
(repeat as above)

Where is Ring Man? Where is Ring Man?
(repeat as above)

Where is Baby? Where is Baby?
(repeat as above)

Where are all the people? Where are all the people?
(repeat as above)

PREPARATION

Draw faces on each of your fingertips with a fine-point marker. Use a glue stick to glue on a little craft hair if desired.

PUPPETRY DIRECTIONS

Tommy Thumb

Pop up each character on cue.

Where Is Thumbkin?

Start with your hand behind your back. On "Here I am" bring out the appropriate finger and wiggle it. On "Run and play" hide your hand behind your back again. To avoid having to hold your middle finger up alone, do not fold the thumb and pointer back down after singing about them. In other words, when you raise a finger keep it raised. Pop them up in this order on cue: thumb, pointer, middle, ring, and pinky.

RELATED BOOKS

Andersen, Hans Christian. *Thumbelina*.

Brown, Marc. *Finger Rhymes*.

———. *Hand Rhymes*.

Cole, Joanna. *Eentsy Weentsy Spider: Fingerplays and Action Rhymes*.

Cooper, Kay. *Too Many Rabbits and Other Fingerplays*.

Galdone, Paul. *The Teeny Tiny Woman: A Ghost Story*.

MacDonald, Margaret Read. *Tom Thumb (The Oryx Multicultural Folktale)*.

Melmed, Laura Krauss. *Little Oh*.

———. *Rainbabies*.

Morimoto, Junko. *The Inch Boy*.

Seuling, Barbara. *The Teeny Tiny Woman*.

Fishes

Five Little Fishes

—Folk rhyme

Five little fishes swimming in a pool.
First one said, "This pool is cool."
Second one said, "This pool is deep."
Third one said, "I think I'll sleep."
Fourth one said, "Let's swim and dip."
Fifth one said, "I see a ship."
The fisherman's line went splish,
    splish, splash,
And away the five little fishes dashed.

Little Fishes

—Folk rhyme

Five little fishes were swimming in a school,
Swimming all around in a cool little pool.
This one said, "I'm as hungry as can be."
This one said, "There's a worm I see."
This one said, "Wait, we better look!"
This one said, "I think it's on a hook!"
This one, so very brave, grabbed a bite and swam away.

PREPARATION

Make five fish. Use different colors.

PUPPETRY DIRECTIONS

Begin the rhymes with your fingers in an upright position. Place each fish on a finger one at a time as you say the rhymes.

Five Little Fishes

Hide your hand behind your back on the last line to indicate that the fish swam away.

RELATED BOOKS

Arnosky, Jim. *Crinkleroot's 25 Fish Every Child Should Know*.

Gomi, Taro. *Where's the Fish?*

Jonas, Ann. *Splash!*

Lionni, Leo. *Swimmy*.

Palmer, Helen. *A Fish Out of Water*.

Pfister, Marcus. *The Rainbow Fish*.

Seuss, Dr. *McElligot's Pool*.

Van Laan, Nancy. *Little Fish, Lost*.

Wu, Norbert. *Fish Faces*.

Five Batty Bats

Five Batty Bats

Bats in the belfry, bats in my hair,
Little mice with wings, flapping through the air.

Five batty bats, rapping at my door,
One flew away, and then there were four.

Four batty bats, hanging from a tree,
One flew away, and then there were three.

Three batty bats, swooping at you,
One flew away, and then there were two.

Two batty bats, fluttering for fun,
One flew away, and then there was one.

One batty bat, left all alone,
One flew away, and then there were none.

PREPARATION

Make five bats.

PUPPETRY DIRECTIONS

Before beginning this poem put all the bats on the fingers. As you recite the poem remove one bat each verse.

RELATED BOOKS

Appelt, Kathi. *Bat Jamboree.*

Cannon, Janell. *Stellaluna.*

Foster, Kelli. *Bat's Surprise.*

Freeman, Don. *Hattie the Backstage Bat.*

Glaser, Linda. *Beautiful Bats.*

Hall, Katy. *Batty Riddles.*

Mayne, William. *Mousewing.*

Milton, Joyce. *Bats: Creatures of the Night.*

Quakenbush, Robert. *Batbaby.*

Ungerer, Tomi. *Rufus.*

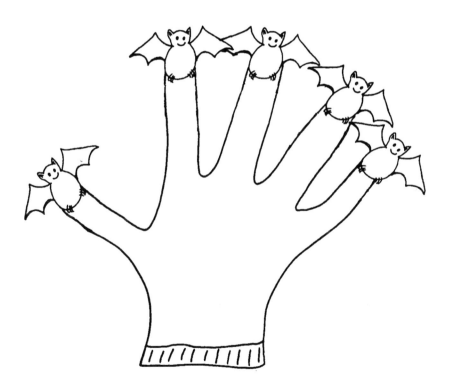

Five in the Bed

Five in the Bed
—Traditional song

(See discograpy for tune)

There were five in the bed,
And the little one said,
"Roll over, roll over."
So they all rolled over,
And one fell out.

There were four in the bed . . .

There were three in the bed . . .

There were two in the bed . . .

There was one in the bed,
And the little one said, "Good Night!"

PREPARATION

Make one puppet from each pattern. Enlarge the bed pattern on a photo-copier and make a bed out of posterboard. Cover it with felt or any other type of cloth.

PUPPETRY DIRECTIONS

As you sing the song hold the bed in front of your gloved hand with the puppets showing on top of the bed. To indicate that the puppets are rolling over simply jostle the puppets a bit. Each time a character falls out of bed fold a finger down. Be sure to put the "little one" on your little finger because you will be folding down your thumb first then your index finger (hold it down with your thumb), your middle finger, and then finally your ring finger. When the "little one" says "Good Night!" gently lean the puppet over to rest on the bed.

RELATED BOOKS

Brown, Margaret Wise. *A Child's Good Night Book.*

Bunting, Eve. *No Nap.*

Campbell, Alison. *Are You Asleep, Rabbit?*

Dale, Penny. *Ten out of Bed.*

Goodspeed, Peter. *A Rhinoceros Wakes Me up in the Morning.*

Inkpen, Mick. *One Bear at Bedtime.*

Robison, Deborah. *No Elephants Allowed.*

Wells, Rosemary. *Good Night, Fred.*

Flowers

Mary, Mary, Quite Contrary
—Mother Goose

Mary, Mary quite contrary,
How does your garden grow?
With silver bells and cockle shells,
And pretty maids all in a row.

Tulips in My Garden
—Folk rhyme

One red tulip in my garden grew,
Up popped another, and that made two.
Two red tulips were all that I could see,
But Mommy found another, and that made three.
Three red tulips, if I could find one more,
I'd put them in a flower vase, and that would
   make four.
Four red tulips, goodness sakes alive,
Oh, here's another one, now that makes five.

Pretty Blossoms
—Folk rhyme

See all the pretty blossoms,
In my garden bed,
The daisies spread their petals wide,
And the tulips bow their heads.

PREPARATION

Make five red tulips and one of each of the other patterns.

PUPPETRY DIRECTIONS

Begin these rhymes with the fingers in an upright position. Place the flowers on the fingers one by one as you say the rhymes.

RELATED BOOKS

Bunting, Eve. *Sunflower House.*
Demi. *The Empty Pot.*
Ehlert, Lois. *Planting a Rainbow.*
Ford, Miela. *My Day in the Garden.*
Gibbons, Gail. *From Seed to Plant.*
Hoban, Julia. *Amy Loves the Sun.*
Lobel, Anita. *Alison's Zinnia.*
Mallet, David. *Inch by Inch: The Garden Song.*

Frogs

Five Green Froggies
—Folk rhyme

Five green froggies sat on the shore,
One went for a swim, and then there were four,
Four green froggies looked out to sea,
One went swimming, and then there were three.
Three green froggies said, "What can we do?"
One jumped in the water, and then there were two.
Two green froggies sat in the sun,
One swam off, and then there was one.
One lonely froggie said, "This is no fun."
It dived in the water, and then there were none.

Five Little Frogs
—Traditional nursery song

(See discography for tune)

Five little speckled frogs,
Sat on a speckled log,
Eating some most delicious bugs.
Yum! Yum!
One jumped into the pool,
Where it was nice and cool,
Then there were four little speckled frogs.
Glub, glub.

(repeat with 4, 3, 2, and 1)

No little speckled frogs.

Froggies on a Lily Pad
—Folk rhyme

Five little froggies sitting on a lily pad.
The first little froggie said, "Let's try to find Dad."
The second little froggie said, "Oh, let's not, let's not.
    I'd rather swim in the swamp."
The third little froggie said, "Swamps are boring.
    I'd rather catch flies before the rain starts pouring."
The fourth little froggie said, "I'd rather soak in the rain,
    catching flies is such a pain."
The last little froggie said, "Let's get out of this pool and
    go to school."

PREPARATION

Make five frogs. Make the log out of poster board.

PUPPETRY DIRECTIONS

Five Green Froggies

Begin this rhyme with the frogs on the fingers. Remove them one by
one according to the rhyme.

Five Little Frogs

Place the frogs on the glove (fingernail side). The back of your hand should be facing front. Hold the poster board log in front of the glove. As you sing the song, fold the fingers down one by one as each frog "jumps in the pool."

Froggies on a Lily Pad

Start this rhyme with the fingers in an upright position. Add each frog to the glove on cue.

RELATED BOOKS

Anderson, Peggy Perry. *Out to Lunch*.

Bancroft, Catherine. *Felix's Hat*.

Faulkner, Keith. *The Wide-Mouthed Frog: A Pop-Up Book*.

Kilborne, Sarah S. *Peach and Blue*.

Lionni, Leo. *It's Mine*.

London, Jonathan. *Froggy's First Kiss*.

Sweeney, Jacqueline. *Once upon a Lily Pad: Froggy Love in Monet's Garden*.

Walsh, Ellen Stoll. *Hop Jump*.

Yolen, Jane. *King Long Shanks*.

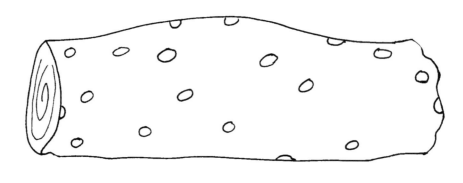

log

The Gingerbread Boy

—Traditional nursery tale

PREPARATION

Make one of each pattern.

PUPPETRY DIRECTIONS

Memorize the story of the "Gingerbread Boy." As each character makes its entrance, place it on the glove. Remove each character when the gingerbread boy runs away from it. The gingerbread boy stays on the glove until the end, when the fox eats him. (Remove him quickly to indicate this.)

RELATED BOOKS

Amoss, Berthe. *The Cajun Gingerbread Boy.*

Cauley, Lorinda Bryan. *The Pancake Boy.*

Egielski, Richard. *The Gingerbread Boy.*

Galdone, Paul. *The Gingerbread Boy.*

Ginsburg, Mirra. *Clay Boy.*

Scieszka, Jon. *The Stinky Cheese Man and Other Fairly Stupid Tales.*

Halloween

Five Furry Bats

Five furry bats were flying by the moon,
"Did you know," said the first,
"Halloween is coming soon?"
"There'll be ghosts!" said the second,
"Floating everywhere!"
"And witches," said the third,
"With green and purple hair."
"There'll be goblins," said the fourth,
"And monsters so I'm told."
"Awesome!" said the fifth,
"Come on, let's go."
Five furry bats flew off out of sight,
And they will all return on Halloween night.

Five Little Pumpkins
—Traditional rhyme

Five little pumpkins sitting on a gate,
First one said, "Oh, my, it's getting late."
Second one said, "There are witches in the air."
Third one said, "I don't care."
Fourth one said, "Let's run and run and run."
Fifth one said, "I'm ready for some fun."
So, ooooooo went the wind,
And out went the light,
And the five little pumpkins
Rolled out of sight!

Five Scary Monsters
—Folk rhyme

Five Scary Monsters on Halloween night,
Made a very spooky sight.
The first monster danced on its tippi-tip-toes.
The second monster tumbled and bumped its
     nose.
The third monster jumped high in the air.
The fourth monster walked like a fuzzy bear.
The fifth monster sang a Halloween song,
Then the five little monsters danced the whole night long.

Three Little Ghostesses
—Traditional rhyme

Three little ghostesses,
Sitting on postesses,
Eating buttered toastesses,
Greasing their fistesses,
Up to their wristesses,
Oh, what beastesses
To make such feastesses!

PREPARATION

Make five each from the bat, pumpkin, and monster patterns. Make
three ghosts and three toasts.

PUPPETRY DIRECTIONS

Five Furry Bats and Five Little Pumpkins

Start the rhymes with the fingers in an upright position. Put each puppet on the glove on cue ("first one said," "second one said," and so on).
Hide the puppets behind your back at the end of the rhymes.

Five Little Monsters

> The directions are the same as for "Five Furry Bats" and "Five Little Pumpkins," except do not hide the puppets at the end. Instead dance your fingers.

Three Little Ghostesses

> Make tiny pieces of toast out of poster board and put double-stick tape on the back. Stick a toast on each ghost as you recite the rhyme.

RELATED BOOKS

Adams, Adrienne. *A Woggle of Witches.*

Apple, Margot. *Sheep Trick or Treat.*

Asch, Frank. *Popcorn.*

Balian, Lorna. *Humbug Witch.*

Johnston, Tony. *The Vanishing Pumpkin.*

Roberts, Bethany. *Halloween Mice.*

Silverman, Erica. *Big Pumpkin.*

Williams, Linda. *The Little Old Lady Who Was Not Afraid of Anything.*

Winters, Kay. *The Teeny Tiny Ghost.*

Ziefert, Harriet. *Who Can Boo the Loudest.*

Hey, Diddle, Diddle

Hey, Diddle, Diddle
—Mother Goose

Hey, diddle, diddle
The cat and the fiddle,
The cow jumped over the moon;
The little dog laughed
To see such sport,
And the dish ran away
    with the spoon.

PREPARATION

Make one of each pattern. Make
the moon out of poster board.

PUPPETRY DIRECTIONS

Start the rhyme with the fingers upright.
Add each figure to the glove as you say
the rhyme. Fold the cat down while the
cow "jumps" over the moon. (Hold the
moon beneath the cow and glide the
cow over it.) Add the other puppets on
cue. Wiggle the dish and spoon on the
last line.

RELATED BOOKS

Brown, Margaret Wise. *Goodnight Moon.*

Choldenko, Gennifer. *Moonstruck: The True Story of the Cow Who Jumped over the Moon.*

De Paola, Tomie. *Hey, Diddle Diddle: And Other Mother Goose Rhymes.*

Eagle, Kim. *Hey, Diddle Diddle.*

Marshall, James. *James Marshall's Mother Goose.*

Hush Little Baby

Hush Little Baby

—Traditional nursery song

(See discography for tune)

Hush little baby, don't say a word,
Mama's gonna buy you a mocking
   bird.

If that mocking bird won't sing,
Mama's gonna buy you a diamond ring.

If that diamond ring turns brass,
Mama's gonna buy you a
   looking glass.

If that looking glass gets broke,
Mama's gonna buy you a billy-goat.

If that billy-goat won't pull,
Mama's gonna buy you a cart and bull.

If that cart and bull turn over,
Mama's gonna buy you a dog named
   Rover.

If that dog named Rover won't bark,
Mama's gonna buy you a horse and cart.

If that horse and cart fall down,
You'll still be the sweetest little baby in
   town.

PREPARATION

Make one of each pattern.

PUPPETRY DIRECTIONS

Add each puppet to the glove to cue the singing. Since there are seven puppets, stick the last two to the palm or back of your glove, whichever is facing the audience. Use double-stick tape on the back of the last two.

RELATED BOOKS

Conrad, Pam. *Animal Lullabies.*
Fox, Mem. *Time for Bed.*
Gerber, Carole. *Hush: A Gaelic Lullaby.*
Halpern, Shari. *Hush, Little Baby.*
Kaye, Buddy. *A You're Adorable.*
Long, Sylvia. *Hush, Little Baby.*
Monrad, Jean. *How Many Kisses Good Night.*
Paxton, Tom. *Jennifer's Rabbit.*
Sharmat, Marjorie. *Go to Sleep, Nicholas Joe.*

Kittens

Three Little Kittens
—Mother Goose

Three little kittens
They lost their mittens,
And they began to cry,
"Oh, Mother dear,
We sadly fear
Our mittens we have
        lost."
"What! Lost your mittens,
You naughty kittens!
Then you shall have no pie.
Mee-ow, mee-ow, mee-ow.
No, you shall have no pie."

The three little kittens
They found their
        mittens,
And they began to cry,
"Oh, Mother dear,
See here, see here,
Our mittens we have found."
"Put on your mittens,
You silly kittens,
And you shall have some pie.
Purr-r, purr-r, purr-r,
Oh, let us have some pie."

The three little kittens
Put on their mittens
And soon ate up the pie;
"Oh, Mother dear,
We greatly fear
Our mittens we have soiled."
"What! Soiled your
    mittens,
You naughty kittens!"
Then they began to
    sigh.

The three little kittens
They washed their
    mittens,
And hung them out to dry;
"Oh, Mother dear,
Did you not hear,
Our mittens we have washed?"
"What! Washed your mittens,
Then you're good kittens,
But I smell a rat close by.
Mee-ow, mee-ow, mee-ow,
I smell a rat close by."

Five Little Kittens
—Folk rhyme

Five little kittens
Sleeping on a chair.
One rolled off,
Leaving four there.

Four little kittens,
One climbed a tree
To look in a bird's nest.
Then there were three.

Three little kittens
Wondering what to do.
One saw a mouse.
Then there were two.

Two little kittens
Playing in the hall.
One little kitten
Chased a red ball.

One little kitten
With fur soft as silk.
Was left all alone
To drink a dish of milk.

This Kitty
—Folk rhyme

This kitty said, "I smell a mouse."
This kitty said, "Let's hunt through the house."
This kitty said, "Let's go creepty creep."
This kitty said, "Is the mouse asleep?"
This kitty said, "Meow, meow,
I saw it go through a hole just now."

PREPARATION

For the "Three Little Kittens" poem cut two layers of felt for each kitten and the mother cat. Put the two layers together and sew around the edges leaving the bottom open so you can fit the cats over your gloved fingers. The front and back of each puppet should be identical (that is, two faces and body fronts) The only difference should be that on one side the kittens are wearing mittens and on the other side they're not. Add wiggle eyes and whiskers. Make the pie out of poster board.

For "Five Little Kittens," make five of the spotted kitten pattern.

PUPPETRY DIRECTIONS

Three Little Kittens

Start with the mittenless side of the kittens facing the audience. Hide the puppets behind your back for a second while they "find" their mittens. Then present the other side of your hand to the audience. Use your free hand to give the kittens the pie.

Five Little Kittens

Begin the rhyme with the kittens on your glove. Remove each kitten at the appropriate time.

This Kitty

Start with your fingers in a upright position. Add each kitten to the glove as you say the rhyme.

RELATED BOOKS

Baker, Keith. *Cat Trick.*

Cauley, Lorinda Bryan. *The Three Little Kittens.*

Gag, Wanda. *Millions of Cats.*

Hersom, Kathleen. *The Copy Cat.*

Hurlimann, Ruth. *The Proud White Cat.*

Kent, Jack. *The Fat Cat.*

Polushkin, Maria. *Who Said Meow?*

Rankin, Joan. *Scaredy Cat.*

Ward, Cindy. *Cookie's Week.*

Leprechauns

This Tiny Leprechaun

This tiny leprechaun all dressed in green,
Is the tiniest man I ever have seen.
This tiny leprechaun so I'm told,
At the end of the rainbow hid all his gold.
This tiny leprechaun has ears that point up.
This tiny leprechaun has lots of good luck.
And this tiny leprechaun for gold does dig,
And he dances a mighty good Irish jig.

Five Little Leprechauns

Five little leprechauns came my way,
On a bright and sunny Saint Patrick's Day.
Down a rainbow they did slide.
And I caught them all before they could
    hide.
"Show me your pot of
    gold!" I cried.
They struggled to get
    away. Oh! How they
    tried.
The first one said, "The
    gold's over there."
The second one said, "No it's
    over here."
The third one said, "We have to
    tell her."
The fourth one said, "Do we?
    Are you sure?"

The fifth one said, "Yes, there's a rule, you see."
The five little leprechauns showed me their gold so bright,
They gave me the pot and said, "Good Night!"

PREPARATION

Make five leprechauns.

PUPPETRY DIRECTIONS

This Tiny Leprechaun

Start this rhyme with your fingers in an upright position. Place the leprechauns on the glove one by one as you recite the rhyme.

Five Little Leprechauns

Start with the puppets on your fingers. As each leprechaun says his line wiggle the appropriate finger.

RELATED BOOKS

Bateman, Teresa. *Leprechaun Gold.*

Blazek, Sarah Kirwan. *A Leprechaun's St. Patrick's Day.*

Chute, Linda. *Clever Tom and the Leprechaun.*

Hanel, Wolfram. *The Gold at the End of the Rainbow.*

McDermott, Gerald. *Tim O'Toole and the Wee Folk.*

Shub, Elizabeth. *Seeing Is Believing.*

The Little Red Hen

PREPARATION

Make one of each. Make the loaf of bread out of poster board with double-stick tape on the back.

PUPPETRY DIRECTIONS

Memorize the story of the "Little Red Hen." Use the Paul Galdone version or one of the many other versions available. Start the story with your fingers in an upright position. As each character makes its entrance, place it on your finger. Stick the loaf of bread on the hen at the end of the story.

RELATED BOOKS

Baker, Keith. *Big Fat Hen.*

Cauley, Lorinda Bryan. *The Cock, the Mouse, and the Little Red Hen.*

Domanska, Janina. *Little Red Hen.*

Galdone, Paul. *Henny Penny.*

———. *The Little Red Hen.*

Hutchins, Pat. *Rosie's Walk.*

Lester, Helen. *The Wizard, the Fairy, and the Magic Chicken.*

Marshall, James. *Wings: A Tale of Two Chickens.*

Mice

Five Little Mice

—Folk rhyme

Five little mice on the kitchen floor
Looking for bread crumbs and something more.
This little mouse peeked behind the door.
This little mouse nibbled at the cake.
This little mouse not a sound did make.
This little mouse took a bite of cheese.
This little mouse heard a kitten sneeze.
"Ah-choo!" sneezed the kitten,
And "Squeak!" they cried,
As they found a hole and ran inside.

This Little Mousie

—Folk rhyme

This little mousie peeked in the door,
This little mousie jumped to the floor.
This little mousie came out to play,
This little mousie ran away.
This little mousie said, "Dear
    me,
Dinner is over, and it's time for
    tea!"

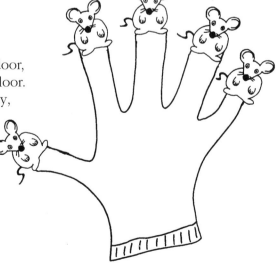

Mouse in a Hole
—Folk rhyme

A mouse lived in a little hole,
Lived softly in a little hole.
When all was quiet as quiet can be . . .
Out popped he!

Hickory, Dickory, Dock
—Mother Goose

(See discography for tune)

Hickory, dickory, dock.
The mouse ran up the clock.
The clock struck one.
The mouse ran down.
Hickory, dickory, dock.

Hickory, dickory, dock.
The mouse ran up the clock.
The clock struck two.
The mouse ran down.
Hickory, dickory, dock.

(repeat with the hours up to twelve)

PREPARATION

Make five mice. Enlarge the clock to ten inches or so. Make it out of poster board.

PUPPETRY DIRECTIONS

Five Little Mice and *This Little Mousie*

Start with your fingers in an upright position. Put each mouse on a finger one by one according to the rhyme. At the end of each rhyme hide the mice behind your back.

Mouse in a Hole

> Place a mouse on your thumb and hide it in your fist. At the end of the rhyme pop it up.

Hickory, Dickory, Dock

> Attach a mouse puppet to a stick or wire, and run it up a poster board grandfather clock. Run the mouse back down the clock on cue as many times as you like, counting off the hours from one to twelve.

RELATED BOOKS

Aylesworth, Jim. *Two Terrible Frights.*

Cauley, Lorinda Bryan. *The Town Mouse and the Country Mouse.*

Henkes, Kevin. *Shelia Rae, the Brave.*

Hutchins, Pat. *Shrinking Mouse.*

Kraus, Robert. *Whose Mouse Are You?*

Numeroff, Laura. *If You Give a Mouse a Cookie.*

Polushkin, Maria. *Mother, Mother, I Want Another.*

Riley, Linnea. *Mouse Mess.*

Yolen, Jane. *Mouse's Birthday.*

Young, Ed. *Mouse Match.*

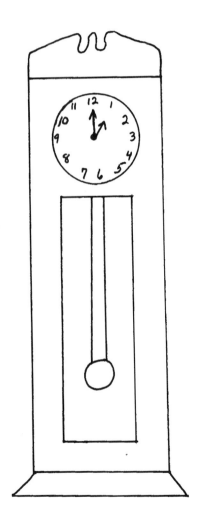

Monkeys

Five Little Monkeys Jumping on the Bed
—Folk rhyme

Five little monkeys jumping on the bed
One fell off and bumped its head.
Mommy called the doctor, and the doctor said,
"No more monkeys jumping on the bed!"

(repeat with 4, 3, 2, and 1)

Put those monkeys straight to bed!

Five Little Monkeys and a Crocodile
—Folk rhyme

Five little monkeys, sitting in a tree,
Teasing Mr. Crocodile: "You can't catch
    me!"
Along comes crocodile quiet
    as can be,
And, SNAP!

(repeat with 4, 3, 2, and 1)

SNAP! Ha, ha, you missed me!

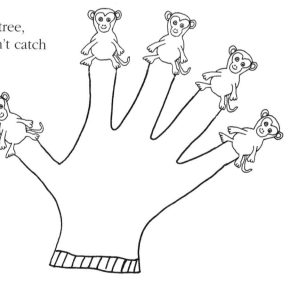

PREPARATION

Make five monkeys. Enlarge the bed pattern and make it out of poster board.

PUPPETRY DIRECTIONS

Five Little Monkeys Jumping on the Bed

Hold the poster board bed in front of your gloved hand with the puppets showing above it. Move the puppets up and down to indicate jumping. Fold one finger down each verse.

Five Little Monkeys and a Crocodile

Start this rhyme with the monkeys on the glove. Remove one monkey each verse. Use your other hand to imitate the snapping motions of a crocodile.

RELATED BOOKS

Bornstein, Ruth. *Little Gorilla.*
Christelow, Eileen. *Five Little Monkeys Jumping on the Bed.*
———. *Five Little Monkeys Sitting in a Tree.*
Galdone, Paul. *The Monkey and the Crocodile.*
Morozumi, Atsuko. *My Friend Gorilla.*
Perkins, Al. *Hand, Hand, Fingers, Thumb.*
Rey, H. A. *Curious George.*
Sierra, Judy. *Counting Crocodiles.*
Van Laan, Nancy. *So Say the Little Monkeys.*
West, Colin. *"Not Me!" Said the Monkey.*

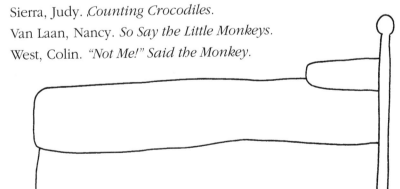

Monsters

Five Scary Monsters
—Adapted folk rhyme

Five scary monsters howling out a roar,
One ran away, and then there were four.
Four scary monsters hiding in a tree,
One fell out, and then there were three.
Three scary monsters eating spider stew,
One got sick, and then there were two.
Two scary monsters having lots of fun,
One ran off, and then there was one.
One scary monster, afraid to be a hero,
He ran away, and then there were zero.

This Little Monster
—Adapted folk rhyme

This little monster went to market.
This little monster stayed home.
This little monster had roast beef.
This little monster had none.
And this little monster went boo, hoo, hoo,
All the way home.

PREPARATION

Make five monsters.

PUPPETRY DIRECTIONS

Five Scary Monsters

Before beginning this rhyme place the puppets on the fingers. As you say the rhyme remove each puppet.

This Little Monster

Begin this rhyme with the fingers in an upright position. Add each monster to the glove one by one as you say the rhyme.

RELATED BOOKS

Brown, Marc. *Monster's Lunchbox.*

Brown, Ruth. *Toad.*

Corentin, Philippe. *Papa!*

Hutchins, Pat. *Silly Billy.*

McPhail, David. *Yesterday I Lost a Sneaker.*

Mayer, Mercer. *There's Something in My Attic.*

Munsinger, Lynn. *One Hungry Monster.*

Sadler, Marilyn. *Alistair Underwater.*

Willis, Jeanne. *The Monster Storm.*

Winthrop, Elizabeth. *Maggie and the Monster.*

The Owl and the Pussy-Cat

The Owl and the Pussy-Cat
—Edward Lear

The Owl and the Pussy-Cat went
    to sea
In a beautiful pea-green boat,
They took some honey, and plenty of
    money
Wrapped up in a five-pound note.
The Owl looked up to the stars above,
And sang to a small guitar,
"O lovely Pussy, O Pussy, my love,
What a beautiful Pussy you are,
    You are,
    You are!
What a beautiful Pussy you are!"

Pussy said to the Owl, "You elegant fowl,
How charmingly sweet you sing!
Oh! let us be married; too long we have tarried:
But what shall we do for a ring?"
They sailed away, for a year and a day,
To the land where the Bong-tree grows;
And there in a wood a Piggy-wig stood,
With a ring at the end of his nose,
    His nose,
    His nose,
With a ring at the end of his nose.

"Dear Pig, are you willing to sell for one shilling
Your ring?" Said the Piggy, "I will."
So they took it away, and were married next day
By the turkey who lives on the hill.
They dined on mince and slices of quince,
Which they ate with a runcible spoon;
And hand in hand, on the edge of the sand,
They danced by the light of the moon,
　　The moon,
　　The moon,
They danced by the light of the moon.

PREPARATION

Make one of each pattern. Make the boat and guitar out of poster board. Put double-stick tape on the back of the props.

PUPPETRY DIRECTIONS

Start the poem with your fingers in an upright position. Put on each puppet as it makes its entrance in the poem. Hold the boat underneath the owl and cat and make a slight wavy motion. Stick the guitar onto the owl at the appropriate time.

RELATED BOOKS

Cole, Babette. *Babette Cole's Cats*.
Hutchins, Pat. *Good-Night Owl*.
Lear, Edward. *The Owl and the Pussy-Cat*.
Voake, Charlotte. *Ginger*.
Waddell, Martin. *Owl Babies*.
Yolen, Jane. *Owl Moon*.

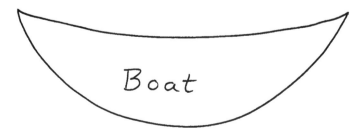
Boat

Penguins

Five Perky Penguins

Five perky penguins,
Stood on the shore.
One went for a swim,
And then there were four.

Four perky penguins,
Looked out to sea.
One went swimming,
And then there were three.

Three perky penguins,
"What can we do?"
One jumped in the water,
And then there were two.

Two perky penguins,
Sat in the sun.
One swam off,
And then there was one.

One perky penguin said,
"This is no fun!"
He dived in the water,
And then there were none.

Five Little Penguins

Five little penguins,
As happy as could be,
Standing on a rock,
Looking out at the sea.

Crash! Went the waves,
Oh, what a din!
Said the first little penguin,
"Shall we all jump in?"

Said the second little penguin,
"The water's like ice."
Said the third little penguin,
"That's not so nice."

Said the fourth little penguin,
"Let's bask in the sun."
Said the fifth little penguin,
"Hey, that's no fun!"

So the five little penguins
Took a leap and a dive,
And splashed into the water,
One, two, three, four, five.

Three seconds later,
Out they popped.
And stood once again,
Atop that big rock.

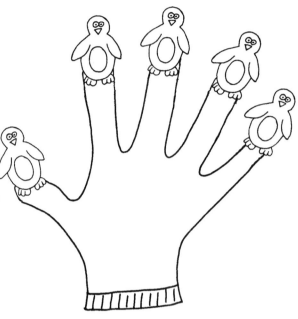

PREPARATION

Make five penguins.

PUPPETRY DIRECTIONS

Five Perky Penguins

Before beginning this rhyme place the penguins on the fingers. As you say the rhyme remove each penguin one at a time.

Five Little Penguins

Start this rhyme with the fingers in an upright position. Add each penguin to the fingers on cue (that is, "said the first, said the second," and so on). On "Took a leap and a dive," fold all the fingers down. On "Out they all popped," pop them up again.

RELATED BOOKS

Alborough, Jez. *Cuddly Dudley.*

Cowcher, Helen. *Antarctica.*

Geraghty, Paul. *Solo.*

Lester, Helen. *Tacky the Penguin.*

———. *Three Cheers for Tacky.*

Murphy, Mary. *I Like It When.*

Perlman, Janet. *Cinderella Penguin: Or, the Little Glass Flipper.*

Pfister, Marcus. *Penguin Pete.*

Wood, Audrey. *The Little Penguin's Tale.*

Pets

My Pets

I have a teeny tiny cat.
Yes, I do. Imagine that.
I love to pet his soft, soft fur.
He loves to play. Just hear him purr.

I have a teeny tiny dog.
When she eats, she's quite a hog,
She grabs her bone and chews
    and chews,
And when she's done, she
    gnaws my shoes.

I have a teeny tiny skunk.
When Mommy saw it, I was sunk.
She said, "Let it go before it sprays!"
Mommy has seen better days.

I have a teeny tiny fish.
A better pet, I couldn't wish,
Her fins are quite a pretty sight,
She keeps on swimming day
    and night.

I have a teeny tiny mouse.
He has a cage for a house.
On his treadmill, he runs fast,
I've shown my pets, and he's the last.

My Five Pets
—Folk rhyme

I have five pets I'd like you to meet.
They live with me on Mulberry Street.
This is my chicken, the smallest of all.
He comes running whenever I call.
This is my duckling who says, "Quack, quack,"
As she shakes water off her back.
This is my rabbit, he runs from his pen.
Then I must put him back again.
This is my kitten, her coat is black and
    white.
She loves to sleep on my pillow at night.
And this is my puppy who has lots of fun.
He chases the others and makes them run.

PREPARATION

Make one of each pattern.

PUPPETRY DIRECTIONS

Start each rhyme with your fingers in an upright position. Place each puppet on a finger one by one as you recite the rhymes.

RELATED BOOKS

Aliki. *At Mary Bloom's*.

Baylor, Byrd. *Amigo*.

Gerstein, Mordicai. *William, Where Are You?*

Johnson, Angela. *Julius*.

Keats, Ezra Jack. *Pet Show!*

Kimmel, Eric A. *I Took My Frog to the Library*.

McPhail, David. *Emma's Pet*.

Seymour, Tres. *I Love My Buzzard*.

Springstubb, Tricia. *The Magic Guinea Pig*.

Wolf, Jake. *Daddy, Could I Have an Elephant?*

Pigs

Five Little Pigs
—Folk rhyme

The first little pig danced a merry, merry jig.
The second little pig ate candy.
The third little pig wore a blue and yellow wig.
The fourth little pig was dandy.
The fifth little pig never grew very big,
And they called him Tiny Little Andy.

This Little Piggy
—Traditional poem

This little piggy went to market.
This little piggy stayed home.
This little piggy ate roast beef.
This little piggy had none.
And this little piggy went,
   "Wee, wee, wee!!"
All the way home.

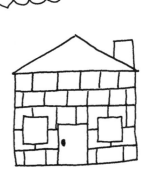

The Three Little Pigs
—Traditional folk tale

Memorize the story of the three little pigs using the Paul Galdone version or one of the many other versions available. Make the three houses out of poster board.

PREPARATION

Make five pigs using a different color of felt for each one.

PUPPETRY DIRECTIONS

Five Little Pigs and This Little Piggy

Begin each of these rhymes with the fingers in an upright position. Put the pigs on the fingers one by one as you recite the rhymes.

The Three Little Pigs

Start this story with the fingers folded down. The back of your glove should face front with the puppets attached to your glove over the fingernails.

Place the first little pig on your index finger and the wolf on your middle finger. Let the first little pig pop up. Hold a poster board cutout of the straw house in front of the pig at the appropriate time. Next, let the wolf pop up. Remove the straw house and pretend the wolf blew it away. Remove the first little pig from your finger to show that the wolf ate him.

Replace the first little pig with the second little pig and perform the same actions using the twig house. To end the story tell how the wolf tried to get in the brick house through the chimney but ended up in the third little pig's cooking pot.

RELATED BOOKS

Axelrod, Amy. *Pigs Will Be Pigs.*

Boland, Janice. *Annabel.*

Galdone, Paul. *The Three Little Pigs.*

Kasza, Keiko. *The Pig's Picnic.*

Keller, Holly. *Geraldine's Blanket.*

McPhail, David. *Pig Pig Grows Up.*

———. *Pigs Ahoy!*

Numeroff, Laura Joffe. *If You Give a Pig a Pancake.*

Oborne, Martine. *Juice the Pig.*

Trivizas, Eugene. *The Three Little Wolves and the Big Bad Pig.*

The Princess and the Pea

—Hans Christian Andersen

PREPARATION

Make one puppet of each pattern. Make the bed out of poster board. (You may want to reverse the bed depending on which hand you use for the princess, so she can lay her head on the pillow.)

PUPPETRY DIRECTIONS

Memorize the story of "The Princess and the Pea." Start the story with the fingers in an upright position. The back of your hand should be facing the audience. This will make it easier to fold the fingers down when needed. Put each character on a finger when they make their entrance during the story. At the appropriate time in the story place the bed underneath the princess puppet letting the finger "lie down" on it. Fold the other puppets down behind the bed when the princess sleeps.

RELATED BOOKS

Andersen, Hans Christian. *The Princess and the Pea.*

Atwood, Eleanor. *Princess Prunella and the Purple Peanut.*

Cole, Babette. *Prince Cinders.*

Inkpen, Mick. *Lullabyhullaballo!*

Karlin, Barbara. *Cinderella.*

Little, Jack. *Once upon a Golden Apple.*

Mann, Pamela. *The Frog Princess.*

Munsch, Robert. *The Paper Bag Princess.*

Thurber, James. *Many Moons.*

Sing a Song of Sixpence

Sing a Song of Sixpence
—Mother Goose

(See discography for tune)

Sing a song of sixpence, a pocket full of rye,
Four-and-twenty blackbirds baked in
 a pie!
When the pie was opened,
The birds began to sing;
Wasn't that a dainty dish to set
 before a king?

The king was in his counting-
 house
Counting out his money;
The queen was in the parlor,
Eating bread and honey.
The maid was in the garden,
Hanging out the clothes;
When down came a blackbird,
And nipped off her nose.

PREPARATION

Make one puppet of each pattern.

PUPPETRY DIRECTIONS

Begin this song with the fingers in an upright position. Put the puppets on the fingers one by one to cue the singing.

RELATED BOOKS

Adams, Pam. *Sing a Song of Sixpence.*

Lee, Dennis. *Alligator Pie.*

Mother Goose. *Over the Moon: A Book of Nursery Rhymes.*

———. *The Random House Book of Mother Goose.*

———. *Songs from Mother Goose: With the Traditional Melody for Each.*

Snow People

Five Fat Snow People
—Adapted folk rhyme

Five fat snow people happy and gay,
The first one said, "What a nice day."
The second one said, "We'll cry no tears."
The third one said, "We'll stay for years."
The fourth one said, "But what happens in May?"
The fifth one said, "Look! We're melting away!"

Five Little Snow People
—Adapted folk rhyme

Five little snow people knocking at my
    door,
One melts away, then there are four.
Four little snow people playing with
    me,
One melts away, then there are three.
Three little snow people playing with you,
One melts away, then there are
    two.
Two little snow people playing in
    the sun,
One melts away, then there is one.
One little snow person when the day
    is done,
Just melts away, then there are none.

Snow People
—Adapted folk rhyme

Five little snow people standing in a row,
Each with a hat and a big red bow.
Out came the sun and stayed all day.
And one of those snow people melted away.

Four little . . .

Three little . . .

Two little . . .

One little snow person dressed for show,
Now that she's ready, where will she go?
When the sun shines, soon she will go
Down through the fields with the melting snow.

PREPARATION

Make five snow people.

PUPPETRY DIRECTIONS

Five Fat Snow People

Start this rhyme with the fingers in an upright position. Place the snow people on the fingers one by one as you recite the rhyme.

Five Little Snow People and Snow People

Before beginning these rhymes place the snow people on the fingers. As you say the rhyme remove each puppet on cue.

RELATED BOOKS

Alborough, Jez. *Ice Cream Bear.*
Briggs, Raymond. *The Snowman.*
Diviny, Sean. *Snow inside the House.*
Ehlert, Lois. *Snowballs.*
Enderle, Judith Ross. *Six Snowy Sheep.*
Evans, Lezlie. *Snow Dance.*
Hoban, Lillian. *Amy Loves the Snow.*
Keats, Ezra Jack. *The Snowy Day.*
Poydar, Nancy. *Snip, Snip, Snow.*
Ziefert, Harriet. *Snow Magic.*

Spiders

Five Furry Spiders

Five furry spiders climbing up the wall,
These furry spiders never ever fall.
The first furry spider said, "Watch me spin!
And then my dinner will soon fly in!"
The second furry spider said, "Did you
    catch a bug?"
The third furry spider said, "I saw one
    beneath the rug."
The fourth furry spider said, "Let's wrap
    it up tight."
The fifth furry spider said, "Don't gobble
    it up! I want a bite!"
Five furry spiders having their dinner,
The bug in the rug was not the winner.

The Eensy Weensy Spider
—Traditional rhyme

(See discography for tune)

The eensy weensy spider
Went up the water spout.
Down came the rain
And washed the spider out.
Out came the sun
And dried up all the rain.
And the eensy weensy spider
Went up the spout again.

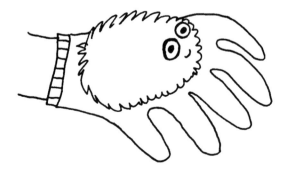

PREPARATION

Five Furry Spiders

Make five spiders.

The Eensy Weensy Spider

Use black craft fur to create the body of the spider. Cut a circle of craft fur and a circle of black felt the same size. Hot glue or sew the edges together leaving a small unjoined area through which you can add stuffing. Glue or sew the fur body (felt side down) onto the back of a tight fitting black glove. Add wiggle eyes.

PUPPETRY DIRECTIONS

Five Furry Spiders

Start this rhyme with the fingers in an upright position. Put the spiders on the fingers one by one as you recite the rhyme.

The Eensy Weensy Spider

Put the puppet on your hand and perform the fingerplay as you normally would.

RELATED BOOKS

Carle, Eric. *The Very Busy Spider.*

Felstead, Cathie. *Creepy Crawlies: Pop-Up Surprises.*

Graham, Margaret Bloy. *Be Nice to Spiders.*

Kimmel, Eric. *Anansi and the Moss-Covered Rock.*

————. *Anansi Goes Fishing.*

Kirk, David. *Miss Spider's New Car.*

————. *Miss Spider's Tea Party.*

MacDonald, Amy. *The Spider Who Created the World.*

Raffi. *Spider on the Floor.*

Trapani, Iza. *The Itsy Bitsy Spider.*

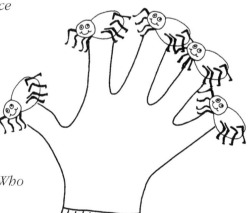

Squirrels

Five Little Squirrels

Five little squirrels playing in the sun,
The first little squirrel said, "Isn't this fun!"
The second little squirrel said, "I see a bear."
The third little squirrel said, "Let's run away from
    here."
The fourth little squirrel said, "Let's hide in the
    shade."
The fifth little squirrel said, "I'm not afraid."
Then "Growl!" went the bear and away they all ran,
Right up the tree!

This Little Squirrel
—Folk rhyme

This little squirrel said, "Let's run
    and play."
This little squirrel said,
    "Let's hunt for
    nuts today."
This little squirrel
    said, "Yes, nuts
    are good."
This little squirrel said,
    "They're our best food."
This little squirrel said, "Come
    climb this tree,
And crack these nuts, one, two,
    three."

PREPARATION

Make five squirrels.

PUPPETRY DIRECTIONS

Start these rhymes with the fingers in an upright position. Add each puppet to the glove on cue. At the end of "Five Little Squirrels" flutter the puppets up your other arm to indicate the squirrels' escape up the tree.

RELATED BOOKS

Alexander, Sue. *There's More . . . Much More.*

Ehlert, Lois. *Nuts to You!*

Kitamura, Satoshi. *Squirrel Is Hungry.*

Lisle, Janet Taylor. *Forest.*

Potter, Beatrix. *The Tale of Squirrel Nutkin.*

Rylant, Cynthia. *Gooseberry Park.*

Schmid, Eleanore. *The Squirrel and the Moon.*

Schumacher, Claire. *Nutty's Picnic.*

Shannon, George. *The Surprise.*

The Three Billy Goats Gruff

—Norwegian folk tale

PREPARATION

Make one puppet of each pattern. Enlarge the bridge pattern on a photocopier and trace it onto poster board.

PUPPETRY DIRECTIONS

Memorize the story of The Three Billy Goats Gruff. I recommend the Paul Galdone version. Place the littlest billy goat on your index finger and the troll on your middle finger. The back of your glove should be toward the audience with the puppets attached to the glove over your fingernails. When you start, the characters should be hidden behind the poster board bridge. Pop up the littlest billy goat and start to tramp him across the bridge. Then pop up the troll. When the littlest billy goat gets across the bridge fold him down, take him off your finger, and replace him with the medium-sized billy goat. Fold the troll down each time he lets a goat cross. Pop him up again as each goat starts to cross. At the end of the story bump the biggest billy goat into the troll puppet and fold the troll down for the last time.

RELATED BOOKS

Galdone, Paul. *The Three Billy Goats Gruff.*

Grimm, Jacob. *The Wolf and the Seven Little Kids.*

Mamet, David. *The Duck and the Goat.*

Roche, Denis. *Brave Georgie Goat.*

Sharmat, Mitchell. *Gregory the Terrible Eater.*

Wolkstein, Diane. *The Banza: A Haitian Story.*

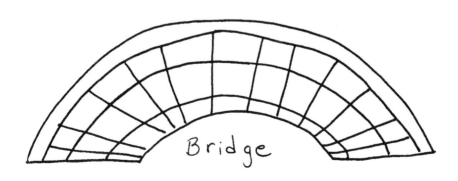

Bridge

Turkeys

Five Fat Turkeys
—Adapted folk rhyme

Five fat turkeys sitting on a fence
First one said, "I'm so immense."
Second one said, "Watch me waddle."
Third one said, "Gobble, gobble, gobble!"
Fourth one said, "Thanksgiving Day is
    coming."
Fifth one said, "Let's start running!"

The turkeys could not be found on
    Thanksgiving Day.
And the old turkey farmer had this to say:
"I guess we'll have pizza."

Five Fat Turkeys Are We
—Traditional song

(See discography for tune)

Five fat turkeys are we.
We slept all night in a tree.
When the cook came around
We couldn't be found.
So that's why we're here, you see.

PREPARATION

Make five turkeys.

PUPPETRY DIRECTIONS

Five Fat Turkeys

Begin the rhyme with your fingers in an upright position. Add each turkey one by one as you say the rhyme.

Five Fat Turkeys Are We

Your hand represents the tree. As you sing the song wiggle the turkeys on the glove.

RELATED BOOKS

Bunting, Eve. *A Turkey for Thanksgiving.*
Child, Lydia Maria. *Over the River and through the Wood.*
Cohen, Miriam. *Don't Eat Too Much Turkey.*
Jackson, Alison. *I Know an Old Lady Who Swallowed a Pie.*
Karr, Kathleen. *The Great Turkey Walk.*
Kraus, Robert. *How Spider Saved Thanksgiving.*
Pilkey, Dav. *Twas the Night before Thanksgiving.*
Schatell, Brian. *Farmer Goff and His Turkey Sam.*
Stock, Catherine. *Thanksgiving Treat.*

Turtles

There Was a Little Turtle
—Vachel Lindsay

There was a little turtle,
He lived in a box,
He swam in a puddle,
He climbed on the rocks.
He snapped at a mosquito,
He snapped at a flea,
He snapped at a minnow,
He snapped at me.
He caught the mosquito,
He caught the flea,
He caught the minnow,
But he didn't catch me.

Here Is My Turtle
—Folk rhyme

Here is my turtle,
She lives in a shell.
She likes her home
Very well.

She pokes her head out
When she wants to eat.
And pulls it back in
When she wants to sleep.

finger

PREPARATION

Make one puppet of each pattern. For "Here Is My Turtle" make the turtle shell out of poster board and the head out of a cut off glove finger. Make two pieces (a top and a bottom). Tape around the edges leaving the front and back of the shell open. Glue on wiggle eyes. Put the turtle head on your index finger and push it through the turtle shell.

PUPPETRY DIRECTIONS

There Was a Little Turtle

Start this poem with your fingers in an upright position. Put on each puppet on cue as you say the rhyme.

Here Is My Turtle

When you recite the rhyme, keep the turtle head tucked in until you say "She pokes her head out." Pull your finger back inside the shell at the end of the rhyme. Repeat the rhyme as many times as you like.

RELATED BOOKS

Asch, Frank. *Turtle Tale.*
Chwast, Seymour. *Mr. Merlin and the Turtle.*
Collins, Pathowery. *Tomorrow, Up and Away!*
Florian, Douglas. *Turtle Day.*
Galdone, Paul. *The Turtle and the Monkey.*
George, William. *Box Turtle at Long Pond.*
Hadithi, Mwenye. *Tricky Tortoise.*
Maris, Ron. *I Wish I Could Fly.*
Stevens, Janet. *The Tortoise and the Hare.*
Stoddard, Sandol. *Turtle Time: A Bedtime Story.*

Valentines

The Valentine Cookies

The cookie jar valentines
Pushed open the lid,
Climbed up the side,
And out they all slid.

They said, "Let's escape!
Let's give it a whirl!
We mustn't be eaten
By that boy or the girl!"

The first little cookie
Opened his red heart eyes
And looked all around the
    kitchen
For a hiding place his size.

The second little cookie
All frosted in pink
Said, "What do we do now?
Let's think, think, think."

The third little cookie
With a candy heart nose
Was so happy to be free
She danced on her toes.

The fourth little cookie
Did a flip and a twist
And slid across the floor,
In a sugary mist.

brad →

Cookies

The fifth little cookie
With frosted blue topping
Said, "I think all our fun
Will soon be stopping."

Because into the kitchen
Came a hungry little boy
There was munching and crunching
And much yummy joy.

The valentine cookies,
I'm sorry to say
Will not be seen again
Until next Valentine's Day!

Five Red Hearts

  —Adapted folk rhyme

Five red hearts from the ten cent store,
I gave one to Willie, now there
    are four.
Four red hearts, pretty ones to
    see,
I gave one to Ellie, now there
    are three.
Three red hearts, with lace and flowers
    blue,
I gave one to Katie, now there are two.
Two red hearts, this is lots of fun,
I gave one to Jesse, now there is one.
One red heart, my story's almost done,
I gave it to Cindy, now there are none.

PREPARATION

Make five red valentines for "The Valentine Cookies." You can use fabric paint for the pink and blue frosting. Make the cookie jar out of poster board and join the corner of the lid to the jar with a brad. Have a boy hand puppet ready for "The Valentine Cookies."

PUPPETRY DIRECTIONS

The Valentine Cookies

Before you begin the poem hide the puppets behind a poster board cookie jar. On "Pushed open the lid" have the puppets push the lid up and peek out. Set the jar aside. Point to or wiggle each puppet on cue. On the line "Came a hungry little boy" bring out a boy hand puppet and have him "nibble" on the cookies. At the end of the poem place the puppets behind your back.

Five Red Hearts

Begin this rhyme with the hearts on your fingers. Remove them one by one.

RELATED BOOKS

Brown, Marc. *Arthur's Valentine.*

Bunting, Eve. *The Valentine Bears.*

Cole, Joanna. *Monster Valentines.*

DeGroat, Diane. *Roses Are Pink and Your Feet Really Stink.*

Gantos, Jack. *Rotten Ralph's Rotten Romance.*

Hurd, Thacher. *Little Mouse's Big Valentine.*

Modell, Frank. *One Zillion Valentines.*

Prelutsky, Jack. *It's Valentine's Day.*

Roberts, Bethany. *Valentine Mice.*

Zolotow, Charlotte. *Hold My Hand.*

Where the Wild
Things Are

PREPARATION

Make four monsters and one boy. Trace the boat pattern onto poster board and cut it out.

PUPPETRY DIRECTIONS

Tell the story *Where the Wild Things Are* by Maurice Sendak. Memorize the story or type the words in reduced size print and glue them to an index card to refer to while you tell the story. Place the Max puppet on your index finger and the monsters on your middle, ring, little finger, and thumb (fingernail side). Your palm should face inward, so when the puppets are folded down they disappear from view. Start the story with Max up and the other puppets folded down. When Max sails off, place the boat in front of him and indicate a slight wavy motion. Make the monsters pop up on "when he came to the place where the wild things are. . . ." Wiggle them around and make monster sounds during the "wild rumpus" and fold them down again when Max sends them to bed. After you finish telling the story with puppets, read the book. The children will love hearing it again.

RELATED BOOKS

Auch, Mary Jane. *Monster Brother.*

Crowe, Robert L. *Clyde Monster.*

Gackenbach, Dick. *Harry and the Terrible Whatzit.*

Hutchins, Pat. *The Very Worst Monster.*

McPhail, David. *The Glerp.*

Mayer, Mercer. *There's a Nightmare in My Closet.*

Nightingale, Sandy. *I'm a Little Monster.*

Ostheeren, Ingrid. *The Blue Monster.*

Sendak, Maurice. *In the Night Kitchen.*

———. *Where the Wild Things Are.*

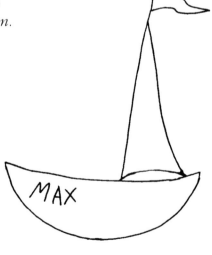

Winter
Animal Friends

Winter Animal Friends

Animal friend, where do you hide
When winter snow covers the ground outside?
I make a snug little home in a hole in a tree
Where I store lots of nuts. It's perfect for me.
Guess who I am.
(a squirrel)

Animal friend, where do you sleep
When the sparkling snow is oh, so deep?
When the snow starts to fall in a cave
   I hide
Where it's warm, snug, and cozy inside.
Guess who I am.
(a bear)

Animal friend, what do you do
When it gets cold and summer is through?
I swim down to the bottom of the pond, you see,
And sleep deep in the mud. It's perfect for me.
Guess who I am.
(a frog)

Animal friend, where do you go
When the wind blows cold and there's ice and snow?
I go where it's warm, I follow the sun.
But I will come back when winter is done.
Guess who I am.
(a bird)

Animal friend, what do you do
When the pond is all ice and you can't see through?
I swim quietly near the bottom without a sound.
In summer I'll stay in the water. I can't walk on ground.
Guess who I am.
(a fish)

PREPARATION

Make one puppet of each pattern.

PUPPETRY DIRECTIONS

Start with your fingers upright. As you recite each verse, ask the children to guess which animal you are describing. Then put the animal on a finger. Repeat this with each animal.

RELATED BOOKS

Brett, Jan. *The Mitten.*
Brown, Margaret Wise. *Animals in the Snow.*
Cartwright, Ann. *The Winter Hedgehog.*
Dabcovich, Lydia. *Sleepy Bear.*
Ezra, Mark. *The Hungry Otter.*
Hasler, Eveline. *Winter Magic.*
Ryder, Joanne. *Chipmunk Song.*
Selsam, Millicent. *Keep Looking!*
Tejima, Keizaburo. *Fox's Dream.*
Yee, Patrick. *Winter Rabbit.*

Winter Holidays

Rudolph the Red-Nosed Reindeer
 —Words and music by Johnny Marks

(See discography)

Here Is the Chimney

—Folk rhyme

Here is the chimney,
Here is the top,
Open the lid,
And out Santa will pop!

Five Little Dreidels

Five little dreidels all in a row,
Spin them, spin them, spin them so.
The first went spinning, oh so fast.
The second one's spinning did not last.
The third one spun across the
    ground.
The fourth one went around and
    around.
The fifth one said, "Look at me!
I'll never stop spinning. Watch and see!"
Five little dreidels all in a row,
Spinning on Hanukkah, just like so.

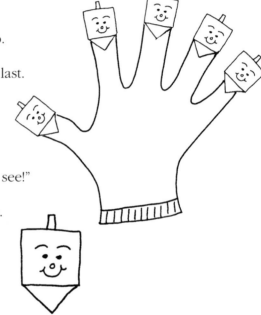

PREPARATION

Make four reindeer and one Santa. Make the sleigh out of poster board. Add tiny bells to the sleigh and reindeer. Glue on a small red bead or pom-pom for Rudolph's nose. Make five dreidels.

PUPPETRY DIRECTIONS

Rudolph the Red-Nosed Reindeer

Use a red or green glove. Begin with your fingers upright. Put Rudolph on your little finger. As you sing the song put on each reindeer and then Santa Claus. Hold the sleigh underneath Santa and make a gliding motion.

Here Is the Chimney

Put Santa on your thumb and hide him inside your fist. Let him pop up at the end of the rhyme.

Five Little Dreidels

Begin with your fingers upright. Place each dreidel on a finger on cue.

RELATED BOOKS

Brown, Margaret Wise. *On Christmas Eve.*

Chocolate, Deborah M. Newton. *My First Kwanzaa Book.*

Harris, Christine. *Oliver All Alone.*

Hill, Eric. *Spot's First Christmas.*

Hoffman, James. *The Christmas Wreath.*

Kajpust, Melissa. *A Dozen Silk Diapers.*

Kimmel, Eric A. *The Magic Dreidels.*

O'Brien, John. *Mother Hubbard's Christmas.*

Price, Moe. *The Reindeer Christmas.*

Schotter, Roni. *Hanukkah!*

Worms

Hermie the Worm

Hermie the worm got hungry one day,
He found a sweet apple and nibbled away.
He nibbled and tunneled
Until the day was done,
And then popped his head out
And said, "Isn't this fun!"

Willie Ate a Worm Today

—Jack Prelutsky

Wiggly Wiggly Worm

(*Tune:* "The Farmer in the Dell," *see discography*)

The wiggly, wiggly worm
The wiggly, wiggly worm
The wiggly, wiggly, wiggly worm
Is wiggling in the apple.

PREPARATION

Make the worm puppet by sewing together two worm-shaped pieces of pink cloth just big enough to fit over your index finger. You may also cut off the finger of a glove for this purpose. Glue on wiggle eyes and a smile. Enlarge the apple pattern on a photocopier and trace it onto poster board. Have a boy hand puppet ready for "Willie Ate a Worm Today."

PUPPETRY DIRECTIONS

Hermie the Worm

Wiggle the worm into the hole in the apple. At the end of the poem, turn your hand and the apple around so the worm pokes out of it.

Willie Ate a Worm Today

Recite "Willie Ate a Worm Today" while wiggling a worm puppet on your index finger. This poem may be found on page 11 in *Rolling Harvey Down the Hill* by Jack Prelutsky. For added drama, put a boy hand puppet on your other hand and have him nibble on the worm.

Wiggly Wiggly Worm

Wiggle the worm through the hole in the apple.

RELATED BOOKS

Lindgren, Barbro. *A Worm's Tale.*

Lionni, Leo. *Inch by Inch.*

O'Callahan, Jay. *Herman and Marguerite: An Earth Story.*

Pelham, David. *Worms Wiggle.*

Pinczes, Elinor. *Inchworm and a Half.*

Seuss, Dr. *The Big Brag.*

Van Laan, Nancy. *The Big Fat Worm.*

Wilson, Jane. *Charlie's Great Escape.*

BIBLIOGRAPHY

Aardema, Verna. *Rabbit Makes a Monkey Out of Lion*. New York: Dial, 1989.

Adams, Adrienne. *A Woggle of Witches*. New York: Scribner, 1971.

Adams, Pam. *Sing a Song of Sixpence*. New York: Child's Play, 1998.

Alborough, Jez. *Cuddly Dudley*. Cambridge, Mass.: Candlewick, 1995.

———. *Ice Cream Bear*. Cambridge, Mass.: Candlewick, 1997.

———. *Where's My Teddy*. Cambridge, Mass.: Candlewick, 1992.

Alexander, Sue. *There's More . . . Much More*. New York: Harcourt, 1987.

Aliki. *At Mary Bloom's*. New York: Greenwillow, 1983.

Allen, Pamela. *Belinda*. New York: Viking, 1992.

Amoss, Berthe. *The Cajun Gingerbread Boy*. New York: Hyperion, 1994.

Andersen, Hans Christian. *The Princess and the Pea*. Boston: Houghton Mifflin, 1979.

———. *Thumbelina*. New York: Doubleday, 1997.

Anderson, Peggy Perry. *Out to Lunch*. Boston: Houghton Mifflin, 1998.

Appelt, Kathi. *Bat Jamboree*. New York: Morrow, 1996.

Apple, Margot. *Sheep Trick or Treat*. Boston: Houghton Mifflin, 1997.

Arnosky, Jim. *All Night Near the Water*. New York: Putnam, 1994.

———. *Crinkleroot's 25 Fish Every Child Should Know*. New York: Simon & Schuster, 1993.

Asch, Frank. *Bear's Bargain*. New York: Aladdin, 1989.

———. *Popcorn*. New York: Parents, 1979.

———. *Turtle Tale*. New York: Dial, 1980.

Atwood, Eleanor. *Princess Prunella and the Purple Peanut*. New York: Workman, 1995.

Auch, Mary Jane. *Easter Egg Farm*. New York: Holiday, 1992.

———. *Monster Brother*. New York: Holiday, 1994.

———. *Peeping Beauty*. New York: Holiday, 1995.

Axelrod, Amy. *Pigs Will Be Pigs*. New York: Simon & Schuster, 1994.

Aylesworth, Jim. *Old Black Fly*. New York: Holt, 1991.

———. *Two Terrible Frights*. New York: Atheneum, 1989.

Baker, Keith. *Big Fat Hen*. New York: Harcourt, 1994.

———. *Cat Trick*. New York: Harcourt, 1997.

Balian, Lorna. *Humbug Witch*. Nashville: Abingdon, 1965.

Bancroft, Catherine. *Felix's Hat*. New York: Simon & Schuster, 1993.

Bateman, Teresa. *Leprechaun Gold*. New York: Holiday, 1998.

Baylor, Bird. *Amigo*. New York: Aladdin, 1989.

Berkowitz, Linda. *Alfonse, Where Are You?* New York: Crown, 1996.

Blazek, Sarah Kirwan. *A Leprechaun's St. Patrick's Day*. New York: Pelican, 1997.

Blume, Karin. *Circus: Funny Fingers*. New York: Abbeville, 1996.

Boland, Janice. *Annabel*. New York: Dial, 1995.

Bornstein, Ruth. *Little Gorilla*. New York: Seabury, 1976.

Brett, Jan. *The Mitten*. New York: Putnam, 1989.

Briggs, Raymond. *The Snowman*. New York: Random House, 1989.

Brown, Ken. *Mucky Pup*. New York: Dutton, 1997.

Brown, Marc. *Arthur's Valentine*. Boston: Little Brown, 1980.

———. *Finger Rhymes*. New York: Dutton, 1988.

———. *Hand Rhymes*. New York: Dutton, 1985.

———. *Monster's Lunchbox*. Boston: Little Brown, 1995.

Brown, Margaret *Wise*. *Animals in the Snow*. New York: Hyperion, 1995.

———. *Big Red Barn*. New York: Harper, 1989.

———. *A Child's Good Night Book*. New York: Harper, 1992.

———. *Goodnight Moon*. New York: Harper, 1947.

———. *On Christmas Eve*. New York: Harper, 1996.

———. *The Runaway Bunny*. New York: Harper, 1942.

Brown, Ruth. *Toad*. New York: Dutton, 1997.

Bunting, Eve. *Ducky*. New York: Clarion, 1997.

———. *No Nap*. New York: Clarion, 1989.

———. *Sunflower House*. New York: Harcourt, 1996.

———. *A Turkey for Thanksgiving*. New York: Clarion, 1991.

———. *The Valentine Bears*. New York: Clarion, 1983.

Burningham, John. *Cannonball Simp*. Cambridge, Mass.: Candlewick, 1994.

Campbell, Alison. *Are You Asleep Rabbit?* New York: Lothrop, 1990.

Cannon, Janell. *Stellaluna*. New York: Harcourt, 1993.

Carle, Eric. *The Grouchy Ladybug*. New York: Harper & Row, 1977.

———. *The Very Busy Spider*. New York: Philomel, 1988.

Cartwright, Ann. *The Winter Hedgehog*. New York: Macmillan, 1990.

Cartwright, Stephen. *Find the Teddy*. London: Usborne, 1983.

Cauley, Lorinda Bryan. *The Cock, the Mouse, and the Little Red Hen*. New York; Putnam, 1982.

———. *The Pancake Boy*. New York: Putnam, 1988.

———. *The Three Little Kittens*. New York: Putnam, 1982.

———. *The Town Mouse and the Country Mouse*. New York: Putnam, 1984.

———. *The Trouble with Tyrannosaurus Rex*. San Diego: Harcourt, 1988.

Child, Lydia Maria. *Over the River and through the Wood.* Boston: Little Brown, 1994.

Chocolate, Deborah M. Newton. *My First Kwanzaa Book.* New York: Scholastic, 1992.

Choldenko, Gennifer. *Moonstruck: The True Story of the Cow Who Jumped over the Moon.* New York: Hyperion, 1996.

Christelow, Eileen. *Five Little Monkeys Jumping on the Bed.* Boston: Houghton Mifflin, 1990.

———. *Five Little Monkeys Sitting in a Tree.* New York: Clarion, 1991.

Chute, Linda. *Clever Tom and the Leprechaun.* New York: Lothrop, 1988.

Chwast, Seymour. *Mr. Merlin and the Turtle.* New York: Greenwillow, 1996.

Cohen, Miriam. *Don't Eat Too Much Turkey.* New York; Greenwillow, 1987.

Cole, Babette. *Babette Cole's Cats.* New York: Warner, 1995.

———. *Prince Cinders.* New York: Putnam, 1988.

Cole, Joanna. *Eentsy Weentsy Spider: Fingerplays and Action Rhymes.* New York: Morrow, 1991.

———. *Monster Valentines.* New York: Scholastic, 1990.

Collins, Pathowery. *Tomorrow, Up and Away!* Boston: Houghton Mifflin, 1990.

Conrad, Pam. *Animal Lullabies.* New York: Harper, 1997.

———. *The Rooster's Gift.* New York: Harper, 1996.

Cooper, Kay. *Too Many Rabbits and Other Fingerplays.* New York: Cartwheel Books, 1995.

Corentin, Philippe. *Papa!* San Francisco: Chronicle, 1997.

Cowcher, Helen. *Antarctica.* New York: Farrar, 1990.

Crowe, Robert L. *Clyde Monster.* New York: Dutton, 1976.

Dabcovich, Lydia. *Ducks Fly.* New York: Dutton, 1990.

———. *Sleepy Bear.* New York: Dutton, 1982.

Dale, Penny. *Ten out of Bed.* Cambridge, Mass.: Candlewick, 1994.

DeGroat, Diane. *Roses Are Pink and Your Feet Really Stink.* New York: Mulberry, 1997.

De Paola, Tomie. *Hey, Diddle Diddle: And Other Mother Goose Rhymes.* New York: Paper Star, 1998.

Delton, Judy. *Two Good Friends.* New York: Crown, 1974.

Demi. *The Empty Pot.* New York: Holt, 1990.

Denim, Sue. *The Dumb Bunnies.* New York: Blue Sky, 1994.

Diviny, Sean. *Snow inside the House.* New York: Harper, 1998.

Domanska, Janina. *Little Red Hen.* New York: Macmillan, 1973.

Drescher, Henrik. *Klutz.* New York: Hyperion, 1996.

Eagle, Kim. *Hey, Diddle Diddle.* Boston: Whispering Coyote, 1997.

Egielski, Richard. *The Gingerbread Boy.* New York: Harper, 1997.

Ehlert, Lois. *Circus.* New York: Harper, 1992.

———. *Color Farm.* New York: Harcourt, 1990.

———. *Feathers for Lunch.* San Diego: Harcourt, 1990.

———. *Nuts to You!* New York: Harcourt, 1993.

———. *Planting a Rainbow.* New York: Harcourt, 1988.

———. *Snowballs.* New York: Harcourt, 1995.

Enderle, Judith Ross. *Six Snowy Sheep.* New York: Boyds Mills, 1994.

Ernst, Lisa Campbell. *Ginger Jumps*. New York: Aladdin, 1996.

———. *Zinnia and Dot*. New York: Viking, 1992.

Evans, Lezlie. *Snow Dance*. Boston: Houghton Mifflin, 1997.

Ezra, Mark. *The Hungry Otter*. New York: Crocodile Books, 1996.

Faulkner, Keith. *The Wide-Mouthed Frog: A Pop-Up Book*. New York: Dial, 1996.

Felstead, Cathie. *Creepy Crawlies: Pop-Up Surprises*. New York: Barrons, 1997.

Flack, Marjorie. *Angus and the Cat*. New York: Farrar, 1997.

Fleming, Denise. *In the Tall, Tall Grass*. New York: Holt, 1991.

Florian, Douglas. *Turtle Day*. New York: Crowell, 1989.

Ford, Miela. *Little Elephant*. New York: Greenwillow, 1994.

———. *My Day in the Garden*. New York: Greenwillow, 1998.

Foster, Kelli. *Bat's Surprise*. New York: Barrons, 1993.

Fox, Mem. *Time for Bed*. New York: Harcourt, 1993.

Freeman, Don. *Bearymore*. New York: Viking, 1976.

———. *Hattie the Backstage Bat*. New York: Viking, 1988.

French, Vivian. *Red Hen and Sly Fox*. New York: Simon & Schuster, 1995.

Gackenbach, Dick. *Harry and the Terrible Whatzit*. New York: Seabury, 1977.

Gag, Wanda. *Millions of Cats*. New York: Coward-McCann, 1928.

Galdone, Paul. *The Gingerbread Boy*. New York: Clarion, 1979.

———. *Henny Penny*. Boston: Houghton Mifflin, 1979.

———. *The Little Red Hen*. New York: Seabury, 1973.

———. *Little Tuppen*. New York: Seabury, 1967.

———. *The Monkey and the Crocodile*. Boston: Houghton Mifflin, 1987.

———. *The Teeny Tiny Woman: A Ghost Story*. New York: Clarion, 1984.

———. *The Three Bears*. New York: Seabury, 1972.

———. *The Three Billy Goats Gruff*. New York: Seabury, 1973.

———. *The Three Little Pigs*. New York: Clarion, 1970.

———. *The Turtle and the Monkey*. New York: Clarion, 1983.

Gantos, Jack. *Rotten Ralph's Rotten Romance*. Boston: Houghton Mifflin, 1997.

George, William. *Box Turtle at Long Pond*. New York: Greenwillow, 1989.

Geraghty, Paul. *Solo*. New York: Crown, 1996.

Gerber, Carole. *Hush: A Gaelic Lullaby*. Boston: Whispering Coyote, 1997.

Gerstein, Mordicai. *William, Where Are You?* New York: Crown, 1985.

Gibbons, Gail. *From Seed to Plant*. New York: Holiday, 1991.

Ginsburg, Mirra. *Across the Stream*. New York: Mulberry, 1991.

———. *The Chick and the Duckling*. New York: Macmillan, 1982.

———. *Clay Boy*. New York: Greenwillow, 1997.

———. *Good Morning, Chick*. New York: Greenwillow, 1980.

Glaser, Linda. *Beautiful Bats*. New York: Millbrook, 1997.

Golembe, Carla. *Dog Magic*. Boston: Houghton Mifflin, 1997.

Gomi, Taro. *Where's the Fish?* New York: Morrow, 1986.

Goodspeed, Peter. *A Rhinoceros Wakes Me up in the Morning*. New York: Bradbury, 1982.

Graham, Margaret Bloy. *Be Nice to Spiders*. New York: Harper, 1967.

———. *Benjy and the Barking Bird*. New York: Harper, 1971.

Grambling, Lois G. *Can I Have a Stegosaurus, Mom? Can I? Please!?* New York: Bridgewater, 1995.

Gregory, Nan. *How Smudge Came.* Custer, Wash.: Orca, 1996.

Grimm, Jacob. *The Wolf and the Seven Little Kids.* New York: North South, 1995.

Hadithi, Mwenye. *Tricky Tortoise.* Boston: Little Brown, 1988.

Hall, Katy. *Batty Riddles.* New York: Dial, 1993.

———. *Buggy Riddles.* New York: Dial, 1986.

Hall, Martin. *Charlie and Tess.* Wauwatosa, Wis.: Little Tiger, 1996.

Halpern, Shari. *Hush, Little Baby.* New York: North South, 1997.

Hanel, Wolfram. *The Gold at the End of the Rainbow.* New York: North South, 1997.

Harris, Christine. *Oliver All Alone.* New York: Dutton, 1994.

Harrison, David L. *When Cows Come Home.* New York: Boyds Mills, 1994.

Hartman, Wendy. *The Dinosaurs Are Back and It's Your Fault, Edward!* New York: McElderry, 1997.

Hasler, Eveline. *Winter Magic.* New York: Morrow, 1984.

Hazen, Barbara. *The New Dog.* New York: Dial, 1997.

Heine, Helme. *The Most Wonderful Egg in the World.* New York: Atheneum, 1983.

Henkes, Kevin. *Shelia Rae, the Brave.* New York: Greenwillow, 1987.

Hersom, Kathleen. *The Copy Cat.* New York: Atheneum, 1989.

Hill, Eric. *Spot Goes to the Farm.* New York: Putnam, 1987.

———. *Spot's First Christmas.* New York: Putnam, 1983.

Hoban, Julia. *Amy Loves the Snow.* New York: Harper, 1989.

———. *Amy Loves the Sun.* New York: Harper, 1988.

Hoban, Lillian. *Arthur's Christmas Cookies.* New York: Harper, 1972.

Hobson, Sally. *Chicken Little.* New York: Simon & Schuster, 1994.

Hoffman, James. *The Christmas Wreath.* Grand Haven, Mich.: School Zone, 1993.

Hooper, Meredith. *A Cow, a Bee, a Cookie and Me.* New York: Kingfisher, 1997.

Hurd, Thacher. *Art Dog.* New York: Harper, 1996.

———. *Little Mouse's Big Valentine.* New York: Harper, 1990.

Hurlimann, Ruth. *The Proud White Cat.* New York: Morrow, 1977.

Hutchins, Pat. *The Doorbell Rang.* New York: Greenwillow, 1986.

———. *Good-Night Owl.* New York: Macmillan, 1972.

———. *Rosie's Walk.* New York: Simon & Schuster, 1968.

———. *Shrinking Mouse.* New York: Greenwillow, 1997.

———. *Silly Billy.* New York: Greenwillow, 1992.

———. *The Very Worst Monster.* New York: Greenwillow, 1985.

Inkpen, Mick. *Lullabyhullaballo!* New York: Artists and Writers Guild, 1994.

———. *One Bear at Bedtime.* Boston: Little Brown, 1988.

Jackson, Alison. *I Know an Old Lady Who Swallowed a Pie.* New York: Dutton, 1997.

Jewell, Nancy. *Snuggle Bunny.* New York: Harper, 1972.

Johnson, Angela. *Julius.* New York: Orchard, 1993.

Johnston, Tony. *The Vanishing Pumpkin.* New York: Putnam, 1983.

Jonas, Ann. *Splash!* New York: Greenwillow, 1995.

Kajpust, Melissa. *A Dozen Silk Diapers.* New York: Hyperion, 1993.

Karlin, Barbara. *Cinderella.* Boston: Little Brown, 1989.

Karr, Kathleen. *The Great Turkey Walk.* New York: Farrar, 1998.

Kasza, Keiko. *A Mother for Choco.* New York: Putnam, 1992.

———. *The Pig's Picnic.* New York: Putnam, 1988.

———. *The Wolf's Chicken Stew.* New York: Putnam, 1987.

Kaye, Buddy. *A You're Adorable.* Cambridge, Mass.: Candlewick, 1996.

Keats, Ezra Jack. *Pet Show!* New York: Aladdin, 1972.

———. *The Snowy Day.* New York: Viking, 1962.

Keller, Holly. *Geraldine's Blanket.* New York: Greenwillow, 1984.

Kennedy, Kim. *Mr. Bumble.* New York: Hyperion, 1997.

Kent, Jack. *The Caterpillar and the Polliwog.* New York: Simon & Schuster, 1982.

———. *The Fat Cat.* New York: Parents, 1971.

———. *Little Peep.* Englewood Cliffs, N.J.: Prentice-Hall, 1981.

Kilborne, Sarah S. *Peach and Blue.* New York: Knopf, 1994.

Kimmel, Eric. *Anansi and the Moss Covered Rock.* New York: Holiday, 1988.

———. *Anansi Goes Fishing.* New York: Holiday, 1992.

———. *I Took My Frog to the Library.* New York: Puffin, 1992.

———. *The Magic Dreidels.* New York: Holiday, 1996.

King, Bob. *Sitting on the Farm.* New York: Orchard. 1992.

Kirk, David. *Miss Spider's New Car.* New York: Scholastic, 1997.

———. *Miss Spider's Tea Party.* New York: Scholastic, 1994.

Kitamura, Satoshi. *Squirrel Is Hungry.* New York: Farrar, 1996.

Kozikowski, Renate. *The Teddy Bear's Picnic.* New York: Aladdin, 1989.

Kraus, Robert. *How Spider Saved Thanksgiving.* New York: Scholastic, 1991.

———. *Whose Mouse Are You?* New York: Macmillan, 1970.

Lear, Edward. *The Owl and the Pussy-Cat.* New York: Clarion, 1989.

Lee, Dennis. *Alligator Pie.* Boston: Houghton Mifflin, 1974.

Lester, Helen. *Tacky the Penguin.* Boston: Houghton Mifflin, 1990.

———. *Three Cheers for Tacky.* Boston: Houghton Mifflin, 1996.

———. *The Wizard, the Fairy, and the Magic Chicken.* New York: Viking, 1988.

Lindgren, Barbro. *Sam's Cookie.* New York: William Morrow, 1988.

———. *A Worm's Tale.* New York: Farrar, 1988.

Lionni, Leo. *Inch by Inch.* New York: Astor-Honor, 1960.

———. *It's Mine.* New York: Knopf, 1986.

———. *Swimmy.* New York: Pantheon, 1963.

Lisle, Janet Taylor. *Forest.* New York: Orchard, 1993.

Little, Jack. *Once upon a Golden Apple.* Markham, Ont.: Viking, 1991.

Lobel, Anita. *Alison's Zinnia.* New York: Greenwillow, 1990.

London, Jonathan. *Froggy's First Kiss.* New York: Viking, 1998.

———. *Little Red Monkey.* New York: Dutton, 1997.

Long, Sylvia. *Hush, Little Baby.* San Francisco: Chronicle, 1997.

McBratney, Sam. *Guess How Much I Love You.* Cambridge, Mass.: Candlewick, 1996.

McDermott, Gerald. *Tim O'Toole and the Wee Folk.* New York: Viking, 1990.

MacDonald, Amy. *The Spider Who Created the World.* New York: Orchard, 1996.

MacDonald, Margaret Read. *Tom Thumb (The Oryx Multicultural Folktale)*. Phoenix: Oryx, 1993.

McDonald, Megan. *Insects Are My Life*. New York: Orchard, 1995.

McDonnell, Flora. *I Love Animals*. Cambridge, Mass.: Candlewick, 1994.

McKee, David. *Elmer*. New York: Lothrop, 1968.

———. *Elmer Again*. New York: Lothrop, 1992.

McPhail, David. *Emma's Pet*. New York: Dutton, 1985.

———. *The Glerp*. Englewood Cliffs, N.J.: Silver, 1995.

———. *Pig Pig Grows Up*. New York: Dutton, 1980.

———. *Pigs Ahoy!* New York: Dutton, 1995.

———. *Yesterday I Lost a Sneaker*. Englewood Cliffs, N.J.: Silver, 1995.

Mallet, David. *Inch by Inch: The Garden Song*. New York: Harper, 1995.

Mamet, David. *The Duck and the Goat*. New York: St. Martins, 1996.

Mann, Pamela. *The Frog Princess*. Milwaukee, Wis.: Gareth Stevens, 1995.

Manzsell, Dom. *My Old Teddy*. Cambridge, Mass.: Candlewick, 1991.

Maris, Ron. *I Wish I Could Fly*. New York: Greenwillow, 1986.

Marshall, James. *James Marshall's Mother Goose*. New York: Farrar, 1979.

———. *Wings: A Tale of Two Chickens*. New York: Viking, 1986.

Marx, Patricia. *Joey T. and the Missing Cookie: A Lift-the-Flap Adventure*. New York: Little Simon, 1997.

Mayer, Mercer. *There's a Nightmare in My Closet*. New York: Dial, 1968.

———. *There's Something in My Attic*. New York: Dial, 1988.

Mayne, William. *Mousewing*. Englewood Cliffs, N.J.: Prentice-Hall, 1987.

Meddaugh, Susan. *Tree of Birds*. Boston: Houghton Mifflin, 1990.

Melmed, Laura Krauss. *Little Oh*. New York: Lothrop, 1997.

———. *Rainbabies*. New York: Lothrop, 1992.

Milton, Joyce. *Bats: Creatures of the Night*. New York: Price, 1993.

Modell, Frank. *One Zillion Valentines*. New York: Morrow, 1987.

Monrad, Jean. *How Many Kisses Good Night*. New York: Random, 1997.

Morimoto, Junko. *The Inch Boy*. New York: Viking, 1988.

Morozumi, Atsuko. *My Friend Gorilla*. New York: Farrar, 1998.

Most, Bernard. *Cock-a-Doddle-Moo!* New York: Harcourt, 1996.

———. *How Big Were the Dinosaurs?* San Diego: Harcourt, 1994.

Mother Goose. *Over the Moon: A Book of Nursery Rhymes*. New York: Clarkson N. Potter, 1985.

———. *The Random House Book of Mother Goose*. New York: Random, 1986.

———. *Songs from Mother Goose: With the Traditional Melody for Each*. New York: Harper, 1989.

Munsch, Robert. *The Paper Bag Princess*. Toronto: Annick, 1980.

Munsinger, Lynn. *One Hungry Monster*. Boston: Little Brown, 1992.

Murphy, Jill. *A Quiet Night In*. Cambridge, Mass.: Candlewick, 1994.

Murphy, Jim. *Dinosaur for a Day*. New York: Scholastic, 1996.

Murphy, Mary. *I Like it When*. San Diego: Harcourt, 1997.

Nightingale, *Sandy. I'm a Little Monster*. San Diego: Harcourt, 1995.

Nodset, Joan L. *Who Took the Farmer's Hat*. New York: Harper, 1963.

Numeroff, Laura Joffe. *If You Give a Mouse a Cookie*. New York: Harper, 1985.

———. *If You Give a Pig a Pancake.* New York: Harper, 1998.

Oborne, Martine. *Juice the Pig.* New York: Holt, 1997.

O'Brien, John. *Mother Hubbard's Christmas.* New York: Boyds Mills, 1996.

O'Callahan, Jay. *Herman and Marguerite: An Earth Story.* New York: Peachtree, 1996.

Ormerod, Jan. *The Story of Chicken Licken.* New York: Lothrop, 1985.

Ostheeren, Ingrid. *The Blue Monster.* New York: North South, 1996.

Palmer, Helen. *A Fish Out of Water.* New York: Beginner Books, 1961.

Paxton, Tom. *Engelbert Joins the Circus.* New York: Morrow, 1997.

———. *Jennifer's Rabbit.* New York: Morrow, 1988.

Peet, Bill. *Chester the Worldly Pig.* Boston: Houghton Mifflin, 1980.

Pelham, David. *Worms Wiggle.* New York: Simon & Schuster, 1988.

Perkins, Al. *Hand, Hand, Fingers, Thumb.* New York: Random, 1978.

Perlman, Janet. *Cinderella Penguin: Or, the Little Glass Flipper.* New York: Viking, 1993.

Pfister, Marcus. *Penguin Pete.* New York: North South, 1989.

———. *The Rainbow Fish.* New York: North South, 1992.

Pilkey, Dav. *The Silly Gooses.* New York: Scholastic, 1998.

———. *Twas the Night before Thanksgiving.* New York: Orchard, 1990.

Pinczes, Elinor. *Inchworm and a Half.* Boston: Houghton Mifflin, 1998.

Polushkin, Maria. *Mother, Mother, I Want Another.* New York: Crown, 1978.

———. *Who Said Meow?* New York: Bradbury, 1988.

Pomerantz, Charlotte. *Here Comes Henny.* New York: Greenwillow, 1994.

Potter, Beatrix. *The Tale of Peter Rabbit.* New York: F. Warne, 1987.

———. *The Tale of Squirrel Nutkin.* New York: F. Warne, 1931.

Poydar, Nancy. *Snip, Snip, Snow.* New York: Holiday, 1997.

Prelutsky, Jack. *It's Valentine's Day.* New York: Greenwillow, 1983.

———. *Rolling Harvey Down the Hill.* New York: Greenwillow, 1980.

Price, Moe. *The Reindeer Christmas.* San Diego: Harcourt, 1993.

Primavera, Elise. *The Three Dots.* New York: Putnam, 1993.

Quakenbush, Robert. *Batbaby.* New York: Random, 1997.

Rader, Laura. *Chicken Little.* New York: Harper, 1998.

Raffi. *Spider on the Floor.* New York: Crown, 1996.

Rankin, Joan. *Scaredy Cat.* New York: McElderry, 1996.

Rey, H. A. *Curious George.* Boston: Houghton Mifflin, 1941.

Rey, Margaret. *Pretzel.* Boston: Houghton Mifflin, 1997.

Riddel, Chris. *The Trouble with Elephants.* New York: Lippincott, 1988.

Riley, Linnea. *Mouse Mess.* New York: Blue Sky, 1997.

Rix, Jamie. *The Last Chocolate Cookie.* Cambridge, Mass.: Candlewick, 1998.

Robart, Rose. *The Cake That Mack Ate.* Boston: Atlantic Monthly Press, 1986.

Roberts, Bethany. *Halloween Mice.* New York: Clarion, 1997.

———. *Valentine Mice.* New York: Clarion, 1998.

Robison, Deborah. *No Elephants Allowed.* New York: Clarion, 1981.

Roche, Denis. *Brave Georgie Goat.* New York: Crown, 1997.

Rosen, Michael. *We're Going on a Bear Hunt*. New York: McElderry, 1989.

Ryder, Joanne. *Chipmunk Song*. New York: Dutton, 1987.

Rylant, Cynthia. *Gooseberry Park*. San Diego: Harcourt, 1995.

Sabuda, Robert. *Cookie Count: A Tasty Pop-Up Book*. New York: Little Simon, 1997.

Sadler, Marilyn. *Alistair Underwater*. New York: Simon & Schuster, 1990.

Schatell, Brian. *Farmer Goff and His Turkey Sam*. New York: Lippincott, 1982.

Schmid, Eleanore. *The Squirrel and the Moon*. New York: North South, 1996.

Schotter, Roni. *Hanukkah!* Boston: Little Brown, 1990.

Schumacher, Claire. *Nutty's Picnic*. New York: Morrow, 1986.

Schwartz, Henry. *How I Captured a Dinosaur*. New York: Orchard, 1989.

Scieszka, Jon. *The Stinky Cheese Man and Other Fairly Stupid Tales*. New York: Viking, 1993.

Selsam, Millicent. *Keep Looking!* New York: Macmillan, 1989.

Sendak, Maurice. *In the Night Kitchen*. New York: Harper, 1970.

———. *Where the Wild Things Are*. New York: Harper, 1963.

Seuling, Barbara. *The Teeny Tiny Woman*. New York: Viking, 1976.

Seuss, Dr. *The Big Brag*. New York: Random, 1998.

———. *McElligot's Pool*. New York: Random, 1966.

Seymour, Tres. *I Love My Buzzard*. New York: Orchard, 1994.

Shannon, George. *The Surprise*. New York: Greenwillow, 1983.

Sharmat, Marjorie. *Go to Sleep, Nicholas Joe*. New York: Harper, 1988.

Sharmat, Mitchell. *Gregory the Terrible Eater*. New York: Simon & Schuster, 1980.

Shub, Elizabeth. *Seeing Is Believing*. New York: Greenwillow, 1994.

Sierra, Judy. *Counting Crocodiles*. New York: Harcourt, 1997.

———. *Good Night, Dinosaurs*. New York: Clarion, 1996.

———. *The Elephant's Wrestling Match*. New York: Lodestar, 1992.

Silverman, Erica. *Big Pumpkin*. New York: Macmillan, 1992.

———. *Don't Fidget a Feather*. New York: Simon & Schuster, 1994.

Simmons, Jane. *Come along, Daisy!* Boston: Little Brown, 1998.

Springstubb, Tricia. *The Magic Guinea Pig*. New York: Morrow, 1982.

Stern, Simon. *The Hobyas: An Old Story*. Englewood Cliffs, N.J.: Prentice-Hall, 1977.

Stevens, Janet. *Tops and Bottoms*. San Diego: Harcourt, 1995.

———. *The Tortoise and the Hare*. New York: Holiday, 1984.

Stock, Catherine. *Thanksgiving Treat*. New York: Bradbury, 1990.

Stoddard, Sandol. *Turtle Time: A Bedtime Story*. Boston: Houghton Mifflin, 1995.

Sweeney, Jacqueline. *Once upon a Lily Pad: Froggy Love in Monet's Garden*. San Francisco: Chronicle, 1996.

Tafuri, Nancy. *Have You Seen My Duckling*. New York: Beech Tree, 1996.

Tejima, Keizaburo. *Fox's Dream*. New York: Philomel, 1987.

Thurber, James. *Many Moons*. New York: Harcourt, 1990.

Tompert, Ann. *Just a Little Bit*. Boston: Houghton Mifflin, 1993.

Torres, Daniel. *Tom*. New York: Viking, 1996.

Trapani, Iza. *The Itsy Bitsy Spider*. Boston: Whispering Coyote, 1993.

Trivizas, Eugene. *The Three Little Wolves and the Big Bad Pig*. New York: McElderry, 1993.

Troughton, Joanna. *How the Birds Changed Their Feathers*. New York: Bedrick, 1986.

Ungerer, Tomi. *Rufus*. New York: Harper, 1961.

Van Allsburg, Chris. *Two Bad Ants*. Boston: Houghton Mifflin, 1988.

Van Laan, Nancy. *The Big Fat Worm*. New York: Knopf, 1987.

———. *Little Fish, Lost*. New York: Atheneum, 1998.

———. *So Say the Little Monkeys*. New York: Random, 1998.

Van Leeuwen, Jean. *Emma Bean*. New York: Dial, 1993.

Verbven, Agnes. *Ducks Like to Swim*. New York: Orchard, 1997.

Vipont, Elfrida. *The Elephant and the Bad Baby*. New York: Coward-McCann, 1969.

Voake, Charlotte. *Ginger*. Cambridge, Mass.: Candlewick, 1997.

Waddell, Martin. *Can't You Sleep, Little Bear?* Cambridge, Mass.: Candlewick, 1988.

———. *Farmer Duck*. Cambridge, Mass.: Candlewick, 1992.

———. *Owl Babies*. Cambridge, Mass.: Candlewick, 1992.

Walsh, Ellen Stoll. *Hop Jump*. San Diego: Harcourt, 1993.

Ward, Cindy. *Cookie's Week*. New York: Putnam, 1988.

Weatherby, Mark Allan. *My Dinosaur*. New York: Scholastic, 1997.

Wellington, Monica. *Mr. Cookie Baker*. New York: Dutton, 1992.

Wells, Rosemary. *Bunny Cakes*. New York: Dial, 1997.

———. *Good Night, Fred*. New York: Dial, 1981.

West, Colin. *"Buzz, Buzz, Buzz," Went Bumblebee*. Cambridge, Mass.: Candlewick, 1996.

———. *"Not Me!" Said the Monkey*. New York: Lippincott, 1988.

Westcott, Nadine Bernard. *Peanut Butter and Jelly*. New York: Puffin, 1994.

Wildsmith, Brian. *The Circus*. New York: Millbrook, 1996.

Williams, Garth. *The Chicken Book*. New York: Delacorte, 1970.

Williams, Linda. *The Little Old Lady Who Was Not Afraid of Anything*. New York: Harper, 1988.

Willis, Jeanne. *The Monster Storm*. New York: Lothrop, 1995.

Wilson, Jane. *Charlie's Great Escape*. New York: Ozark, 1996.

Winters, Kay. *The Teeny Tiny Ghost*. New York: Harper, 1997.

Winthrop, Elizabeth. *Maggie and the Monster*. New York: Holiday, 1988.

Wolf, Jake. *Daddy, Could I Have an Elephant?* New York: Greenwillow, 1996.

Wolkstein, Diane. *The Banza: A Haitian Story*. New York: Dial, 1981.

Wood, Audrey. *Birdsong*. New York: Harcourt, 1997.

———. *The Little Penguin's Tale*. New York: Harcourt, 1989.

Wood, Jakki. *Moo, Moo, Brown Cow*. New York: Harcourt, 1992.

Wu, Norbert. *Fish Faces*. New York: Holt, 1993.

Yee, Patrick. *Winter Rabbit*. New York: Viking, 1994.

Yolen, Jane. *King Long Shanks*. San Diego: Harcourt, 1998.

———. *Mouse's Birthday*. New York: Putnam, 1993.

———. *Owl Moon*. New York: Philomel, 1987.

Yoshi. *Butterfly Hunt*. New York: Simon & Schuster, 1990.

Young, Ed. *Mouse Match*. New York: Harcourt, 1997.

———. *Seven Blind Mice*. New York: Philomel, 1992.

Young, Ruth. *Golden Bear*. New York: Viking, 1992.

Ziefert, Harriet. *Snow Magic*. New York: Viking, 1988.

———. *Who Can Boo the Loudest*. New York: Harper, 1990.

Zion, Gene. *Harry the Dirty Dog*. New York: Harper, 1956.

Zolotow, Charlotte. *Hold My Hand*. New York: Harper, 1972.

———. *Mr. Rabbit and the Lovely Present*. New York: Harper, 1962.

DISCOGRAPHY OF SONGS AND TUNES

"Baby Bumble Bee." *Wee Sing Silly Songs*. Price, Stern, Sloan, 1986.

"The Eensy Weensy Spider." Sharon, Lois, and Bram. *Mainly Mother Goose*. Elephant Records, 1984.

"Farmer in the Dell." *Wee Sing and Play*. Price, Stern, Sloan, 1986.

"Fiddle-I-Fee." *Jokes, Riddles, & Silly Songs*. Golden, 1989.

"Five Brown Teddies." (Tune: "Ten Green Bottles.") Coombe, Rosina. *How Much Is That Doggie?* Storyteller Cassettes Ltd., 1990.

"Five Fat Turkeys." Schiller, Pam. *Where Is Thumbkin?* Kimbo Educational, 1996.

"Five in the Bed." (Tune: "Ten in the Bed.") Arnold, Linda. *Sing Along Stew*. A & M Records, 1995.

"Five Little Ducks." Raffi. *Rise and Shine*. MCA Records, 1982.

"Five Little Frogs." Raffi. *Singable Songs for the Very Young*. MCA Records, 1976.

"How Much Is That Doggie in the Window?" *How Much Is That Doggie?* Storyteller Cassettes Ltd., 1990.

"Hickory, Dickory, Dock." *Old MacDonald Had a Farm and Other Favorite Animal Songs*. Warner Brothers Records, 1992.

"Hush, Little Baby." *Wee Sing Nursery Rhymes & Lullabies*. Price, Stern, Sloan, 1985.

"I Had a Little Rooster." *Old MacDonald Had a Farm and Other Favorite Animal Songs*. Warner Brothers Records, 1992.

"Rudolph the Red-Nosed Reindeer." Clayderman, Richard. *Christmas*. Quality Records, 1990.

"Sing-a-Song of Sixpence." *Wee Sing King Cole's Party*. Price, Stern, Sloan, 1987.

"Where Has My Little Dog Gone?" *Old MacDonald Had a Farm and Other Favorite Animal Songs*. Warner Brothers Records, 1992.

"Where Is Thumbkin?" Schiller, Pam. *Where Is Thumbkin?* Kimbo Educational, 1996.

Diane Briggs is a youth services librarian at the Bethlehem Public Library in Delmar, New York; a school media specialist at the Maplewood School in Watervliet, New York; and a member of the National Storytelling Association. A graduate of the School of Information Science at the State University of New York at Albany, Briggs is also the author of *52 Programs for Preschoolers: The Librarian's Year-Round Planner* published by ALA Editions. Other titles by Briggs are *Toddler Storytime Programs* and *Flannel Board Fun,* both published by Scarecrow Press. She lives in Delmar, New York, with her husband, Scott, and son, Thomas.